Stafford Ransome

Japan in transition

a comparative study of the progress, policy, and methods of the Japanese since

their war with China

Stafford Ransome

Japan in transition
a comparative study of the progress, policy, and methods of the Japanese since their war with China

ISBN/EAN: 9783744738149

Printed in Europe, USA, Canada, Australia, Japan

Cover: Foto ©ninafisch / pixelio.de

More available books at **www.hansebooks.com**

JAPAN
IN TRANSITION

*A COMPARATIVE STUDY OF THE PROGRESS
POLICY, AND METHODS OF THE JAPANESE
SINCE THEIR WAR WITH CHINA*

BY

STAFFORD RANSOME

MEMBER OF THE INSTITUTION OF CIVIL ENGINEERS; RECENTLY
SPECIAL CORRESPONDENT OF THE *MORNING POST*
IN THE FAR EAST

WITH FOUR SPECIAL MAPS BY THE AUTHOR

AND ILLUSTRATIONS

NEW YORK AND LONDON
HARPER & BROTHERS PUBLISHERS
1899

CONTENTS

CHAP.		PAGE
	INTRODUCTION	ix
I.	POPULAR MISCONCEPTIONS OF JAPAN	1
II.	TRAVELLING AND ACCOMMODATION	16
III.	THE STANDING OF THE FOREIGNER	46
IV.	PRESENT DAY EDUCATION	62
V.	THE NEW SCHOOL OF DRAMA	86
VI.	THE POSITION AND PROSPECTS OF CHRISTIANITY	99
VII.	THE MORAL STANDARD	115
VIII.	THE COMMERCIAL INTEGRITY OF THE JAPANESE	128
IX.	INTERNATIONAL BUSINESS RELATIONS	145
X.	MODERN INDUSTRIAL JAPAN	163
XI.	THE EFFECT OF THE WAR ON FOREIGN RELATIONS	179
XII.	POLITICS IN THE PAST AND PRESENT	191
XIII.	OUTLINE OF STRATEGICAL GEOGRAPHY	205
XIV.	THE QUESTION OF COLONIZATION	217
XV.	JAPAN AS AN ALLY	238
XVI.	OUR PROSPECTS UNDER THE REVISED TREATIES	250

ILLUSTRATIONS

	PAGE
THE OLD AND THE NEW JAPAN CONTRASTED . . . . . *Frontispiece*	
A GEISHA AT HOME . . . . *Facing p.*	4
A GEISHA ORCHESTRA. . . . . "	6
A TOKIO DANCING-GIRL . . . . "	8
THE JAPANESE BATTLE-SHIP *SHIKISHIMA* . . . . . . "	12
A SNAP-SHOT IN A VILLAGE STREET . . . . "	20
THE REMAINS OF THE VILLAGE OF SHIMIDZU AFTER A FLOOD . . . . HAKODATE HARBOR, IN THE HOKKAIDO. . . . . . "	24
A JAPANESE HOTEL, INTERIOR . . . . "	26
A TEA-HOUSE, INTERIOR . . . . "	28
COUNT OKUMA . . . . "	60
VISCOUNT YOZO YAMAO* . . . . "	64
THE ENGINEERING COLLEGE OF THE IMPERIAL UNIVERSITY OF TOKIO* . . . . THE LAW COLLEGE AND LIBRARY OF THE IMPERIAL UNIVERSITY OF TOKIO* . . . . . . "	70
THE SCIENCE COLLEGE OF THE IMPERIAL UNIVERSITY OF TOKIO* . . . . IN THE QUADRANGLE OF THE ENGINEERING COLLEGE OF THE IMPERIAL UNIVERSITY OF TOKIO* "	74
MR. FUKASAWA YAKICHI . . . . KAWAKAMI OTOJIRO . . . . "	78
A GROUP OF ENGINEERING STUDENTS AT THE IMPERIAL UNIVERSITY OF TOKIO* . . . . "	82
ICHIKAWA DANJURO . . . . "	88
DANJURO AS THE CHIEF OF THE FORTY-SEVEN RONINS . . "	94
ACTRESS IN OLD-STYLE PLAY . . . . "	96
GIRLS IN GARDEN . . . . "	116

ILLUSTRATIONS

LADY PLAYING THE KOTO	Facing p.	118
AN ACTOR DRESSED AS A YOSHIWARA WOMAN	"	120
TREATY-PORT GIRLS	"	122
PONTA, A TOKIO GEISHA	"	124
THE OFFICES OF THE DEPARTMENT OF AGRICULTURE AND COMMERCE*	"	164
H.I.H. THE LATE PRINCE SANJO VISCOUNT YENOMOTO	"	166
BARON ITO BARON NISHI	"	168
SHIMBASHI RAILWAY STATION, TOKIO MITSU BISHI BANK	"	170
THE NAGASAKI SHIP-BUILDING WORKS	"	176
H.I.H. THE LATE PRINCE ARISUGAWA	"	180
THE MARQUIS ITO	"	184
THE LATE LIEUTENANT-GENERAL YAMAJI COUNT ITAGAKI	"	188
COUNT INOUYE	"	196
OFFICE OF THE *KOKUMIN SHIMBUN* (*THE NATION*, A DAILY PAPER), TOKIO	"	198
THE OFFICE OF THE *NICHI NICHI SHIMBUN* (*DAY-BY-DAY* NEWSPAPER), TOKIO	"	200
H.I.H. THE LATE PRINCE KITASHIRAKAWA COUNT MATSUKATA	"	202
THE MARQUIS SAIGO VISCOUNT YOSHIKAWA	"	204
ADMIRAL NIREI MARSHAL OYAMA	"	206
OFFICES OF THE GENERAL STAFF OF THE ARMY, TOKIO	"	208
THE IMPERIAL NAVAL DOCKYARD, YOKOSUKA*	"	210
THE NAGASAKI DOCK	"	214
JAPANESE MOUNTAIN ARTILLERY APPROACHING PORT ARTHUR DURING THE WAR WITH CHINA	"	238
VISCOUNT KATSURA MARSHAL NOZU	"	244
OLD-STYLE WARFARE (TWELFTH CENTURY). TAKEDA SHINGEN ATTACKING MOUNT MINOBU	"	248

NOTE.—The Illustrations marked * have been reproduced by the permission of the editor of the *Engineer*.

SPECIAL MAPS
PREPARED BY THE AUTHOR

EDUCATIONAL SKETCH MAP . . . . *Facing p.* 70
STRATEGICAL SKETCH MAP . . . . " 198
SKETCH MAP REFERRING TO THE COLONIAL PROSPECTS OF JAPAN . . 225
EMPIRE OF JAPAN . . . . *At end of book*

INTRODUCTION

THERE are three distinct Japans in existence side by side to-day—the old Japan, which has not wholly died out; the new Japan, which as yet has hardly been born, except in the spirit; and the transition Japan, which is passing through its most critical throes just now.

Every one of the three affords an extremely difficult study; and, of them all, that which is the subject of this book is perhaps the most complicated.

The old Japan, in practically all its phases, has been thoroughly thrashed out by many competent writers, several of whom are recognized authorities upon the subject; and had the Japan of to-day received the same careful consideration and able handling as the Japan of the past, there would be but little reason for bringing out this book.

It is true that certain of the writers on the old Japan have added, in the recent editions of their books, chapters touching on the more modern aspects of the country. But the alterations in Japanese methods have been so marked that it is impossible to exhaust the subject satisfactorily in that way.

INTRODUCTION

Vastly interesting as is the old Japan, transition Japan is, in its way, hardly less so, though possibly the subject may appeal to a different reading public. But the two are so completely distinct that, in order to do justice to the one or to the other, they must be treated separately.

The process of transition has been so abrupt that the reader is shocked when, at the end of a bulky volume, dealing with Daimios, flower ceremonies, cherry blossoms, tea-gardens, and temples, he finds these subjects suddenly replaced by modern ordnance, railways, international politics, electricity, and merchant firms. The contrast is too striking to be either artistic or satisfactory.

On the subject of all matters Japanese the local foreigners resident in Japan are so clearly divided into two camps that there is always an endeavor to class a writer on Japan in one of two categories. He is stated either to be "pro-Japanese" or "anti-Japanese." If an author allows a knowledge of that fact to affect his writings, his book is bound to be colorless. If, on the other hand, he steers his own course, and in dealing with his subject frankly gives his impressions for what they are worth, he is bound to say something from time to time to which certain people may take exception; for if a particular point of view should meet with the approval of one section of the community, another section will certainly disapprove of it.

I have adopted the latter alternative in writing this book—that is to say, I have given my own

INTRODUCTION

opinions without any attempt at hedging; and while I sometimes have had occasion to quote other writers either for the purpose of accentuating a theory or a fact, or of explaining the manner in which my own opinions differ from theirs, I have done so with all due deference to their point of view.

So much has been written of one sort and another about Japan that a writer, in almost everything he says, is likely to be plagiarizing or contradicting one or another authority; and in endeavoring to throw light on the chaotic problem of Japanese methods his book is almost bound to appear somewhat controversial and argumentative.

Japan in Transition is merely, as its name implies, a book dealing with the changes which are going on in the country just now; and I describe it by the sub-title as being "a Comparative Study of the Progress, Policy, and Methods of the Japanese since their War with China," not because comparisons are made between the Japan of to-day and the Japan of the past; for in cases where contrasts of that sort have a place in this book they are only incidental. The comparisons made are between the methods of the Japanese to-day and the methods of the people in other countries, in view of the fact that Japan is endeavoring to bring herself into line with the most advanced nations of the earth.

In drawing these comparisons, I have not imagined an ideal Englishman, an ideal Frenchman, or an ideal American, nor a combined ideal made up of the three; I have not taken for granted an as-

INTRODUCTION

sumption that we all act up to our theoretical standards of probity, morality, and enlightenment; nor, in cases where Japanese methods deviate from our own, that such deviations must necessarily place the Japanese in the wrong. I have endeavored to contrast and compare the ordinary methods of the modern Japanese with the ordinary methods of the men one finds elsewhere in the civilized world.

I cannot claim that my book is the result of a sojourn of many years in the country, as I lived in Japan for less than two years (part of 1896, and the whole of 1897). That time, however, was a very critical epoch for the people of Japan, in that the national delirium which inevitably follows a successful war was gradually subsiding, and the country on its new lines, and endowed with its well earned but newly born prestige, was beginning to feel its feet.

When living in the country I held a mixed mandate from two journals—the *Morning Post*, for which I had to write a series of articles on "Japan Since the War," dealing with the effect of the war on that country politically and socially; and the *Engineer*, in the columns of which I was pointing out the engineering and industrial progress of Japan. The present book summarizes, in a form less ephemeral than must be adopted in journalism, the impressions which I received during the time I was carrying on that work.

In *Japan in Transition* I have naturally had to go over a great deal of the ground covered by my former articles; and, by the courtesy of the Editor

INTRODUCTION

of the *Morning Post*, I have been allowed to draw somewhat freely on three of my articles on "Japan Since the War" in writing the chapters on Politics, Morals, and the Drama.

I have to thank the Editor of the *Engineer* for allowing me to use certain photographs—notably those representing the Yokosuka Dock-yard, a group of students, and the Educational Buildings of the Imperial University—which served to illustrate certain of my articles in that journal.

To my friend Professor C. D. West, of the Imperial University, I am indebted for several of the photographs used in illustrating this book; as also to Mr. Y. Fukai, of the *Kokumin Shimbun*, who procured for me many of the portraits which appear in these pages.

I would also take this opportunity of thanking my many friends, both European and Japanese, who so kindly assisted me with their advice when I was working up my subject in that country.

Of that subject I can only say, speaking as one whose branch of journalism has nearly always been that of a foreign correspondent, and whose particular work has usually had to do with the investigation and summing up of complicated situations in various parts of the world, that Japan, at any time, is as difficult a country to write about as one can find, and that the existing conditions of that country render the task of giving a satisfactory account of it especially arduous.

As the chapters in this book deal with so wide a

INTRODUCTION

range of subjects, and as all sorts of side issues come into the question from time to time, it is, perhaps, well briefly to summarize here the line of argument taken in this book. I am a firm believer in the solid nature of the modern progress made by the Japanese—politically, commercially, and industrially. Socially speaking, I think their old methods suited them better than those imported from the West. Their moral instincts, though not based at all on Western theories, are not, as a rule, of a lower order than the average standard of the European nations. They are, as a rule, lacking in that quality known as modern business integrity; but I think this is largely due to a misconception as to the fundamental principles which guide the conduct of modern business.

In the ordinary transactions of life, at all events away from the treaty-ports, the Japanese are still particularly honest, even when dealing with foreigners.

I think that in spite of certain failings, pointed out in due course in this book, the politicians of Japan, generally speaking, and particularly those who are at the head of affairs, keep their hands cleaner than do their *confrères* in many of the countries which boast of a higher civilization.

I believe that, so far as the interests of various countries can be the same, those of Great Britain, the United States, and Japan are, and must be, for many years to come, identical so far as a Far Eastern policy is concerned; for those three Powers are

INTRODUCTION

alone in disapproving of the dismemberment of China, and in respecting international law in that part of the world.

A triple alliance of these three nations would be invaluable in the interests of Far Eastern commerce and peace; and there is no doubt that we should find in the Japanese not only efficient but perfectly honorable allies.

I consider the most marked *trait* in the Japanese character to be their feverish anxiety to acquire, and wonderful capacity for absorbing, knowledge of any sort; and I take a more optimistic view than many well-known authorities with regard to their capabilities for giving practical effect to such knowledge.

Certain writers, presumably basing their standpoint on the many mistakes made by the Japanese in the application of their modern methods, have often assumed that the Japanese are not so efficient in practice as they are in theory. This is so at the present day. I do not think, however, that practical capacity is wanting, but rather that, at their present educational stage, they have not been able to give as much attention to the practical side of their modern training as to the theoretical.

In the rush for modern knowledge it was a question, not as to what would be the best subjects to devote their attention to, but as to which among those subjects could be omitted with the least inconvenience; consequently, practice has been temporarily shelved in favor of the headlong pursuit of theory.

INTRODUCTION

The Japanese are credited, and possibly with perfect justice, with possessing the quality of self-confidence to a somewhat exaggerated degree. Well, assuming that such is the case, I do not think that we can logically censure them on this account. For, after all, self-confidence is a good old Anglo-Saxon vice, and it is to be presumed that neither Englishmen nor Americans would be unjust enough to maintain that it was precisely their lack of this particular characteristic that has enabled them to make of Great Britain and the United States the two most progressive and industrially important countries in the world.

JAPAN IN TRANSITION

JAPAN
IN TRANSITION

CHAPTER I

POPULAR MISCONCEPTIONS OF JAPAN

THERE is perhaps no country in the world which has been more misrepresented by the foreigner to the foreigner than has the Land of the Rising Sun, and the reasons for this are very obvious. Japan is at once the most difficult country to analyze accurately, and the most easy to write about superficially.

The journalist who, after a six hours' sojourn there, has not already been able to find something which would pass muster as interesting "copy," must indeed be a poor hand at his trade; though whether articles written under such conditions are likely to be of any value to the student is a matter of conjecture.

Japan appears to exercise some mysterious influence which not only attracts the pen of the amateur, but which seems to have the effect of drawing the professional writer out of his legitimate element.

Thus the poet, on arriving in that country, suddenly becomes an exponent of character; the theatrical critic a censor of morals; the religious tract-maker an authority on art; and the compiler of railway "puffs" a novelist.

Some of the books thus turned out have occasionally been interesting enough to readers who have no knowledge of the country; and, as occasionally the writers in question have been well known in other spheres of literature, their books have sometimes met with a more ready sale than has been the case with many of the valuable works written by real students of Japan.

Under such circumstances it is only natural that foreigners generally should often imbibe weird and distorted notions with regard to the Japanese character; and the more especially as these writers have frequently based their notions of Japan and the Japanese on what they have seen in the treaty-ports.

Now life in the treaty-ports is so absolutely unlike the life in any other parts of the country that hardly any particulars of the former will be likely to hold good with regard to the latter. It would be just as reasonable to describe a book dealing with "life in Gibraltar" as an exhaustive treatise on Spain, as it is, when reading books about treaty-port doings, to accept them as throwing any light whatever on Japan proper.

Treaty-port people, and especially treaty-port journals, tell us that all Japanese are bad. Well, once upon a time a very learned monarch said in his wrath that all men were liars; and it is probable that the one sweeping statement is as accurate as the other; for the treaty-port resident is in a continual state of wrath, or rather of irritation, with regard to Japanese matters. His interests in the country being, as a rule, purely of a commercial nature, he is naturally somewhat sore when he finds that the new generation of Japanese are increasingly able to carry on their trade without his assistance. For there is no doubt that the treaty-port foreigner in days gone by created and built up the international trade of the country; and he is perhaps right in his estimate of the treaty-port Japanese with whom he comes in daily contact.

In order to understand the position, let us try and imagine that there is established in England a treaty-port, say at Wapping Old Stairs, or other convenient locality for shipping; and that in pursuit of their business a highly respectable class of Japanese tradesmen have established themselves there; that they have built their own houses, live their own lives, wear their own clothes, are under their own jurisdiction, and do not bother to learn our language (for the treaty-port foreigner in Japan, with very rare exceptions, never troubles to learn Japanese). Let us further assume that this imaginary Japanese community in England are in the habit of publishing daily newspapers violently denouncing everything that is British, simply because the methods of the English dock-laborers, cabmen, interpreters, and runners, who hang around their settlement for the purpose of getting what they can out of the residents, are not particularly scrupulous or high-minded. We should say at once that the criticism was unfair, and that the Japanese at Wapping were not in a position to form an accurate estimate of England and the English; that they were basing their opinions of the former on a place which, by reason of its being outside British jurisdiction, was really not England at all; and, of the latter, on people who could not be looked upon as representative specimens of English people generally. We should add that very few respectable Englishmen, if they could afford to do otherwise, would care to live in Wapping under treaty-port conditions, as they would prefer residing among their compatriots in a part of England where extra-territoriality did not exist.

If we transpose this picture, we shall find that it holds good in Japan to-day. The better class Japanese never live in the treaty-ports of that country if they can possibly do otherwise. And it is on account of all these conditions that the treaty-port estimate of Japanese character and methods is misleading.

The freshly arrived foreigner, however, is bound to base his first impressions of Japan on treaty-port surroundings, as he naturally lands at one or other of these places, and very often practically gets no farther during his stay; or, if he does, his journeying merely takes the form of flying trips to the stereotyped places in the interior, where treaty-port people and tourists go; and he gravitates back to, and

A GEISHA AT HOME

By the GENROKU-KWAN

makes his headquarters within, concession limits in one of the coast towns, where he finds the greatest number of his countrymen, the greatest selection of Western amusements, the best quarters, and the best food; and where, above all, he can make himself understood.

Most people who visit Japan arrange their sojourn in that country on the lines just described; and the man who does will tell his friends his impressions as seen through treaty-port spectacles. He will say that the Japanese are devoid of integrity and morality; that they are grasping, unreliable, rude, and even dangerous. For he has read this every day in his treaty-port journal; and he has been overcharged by his treaty-port rikisha boy, who is possibly the most reputable sample of a Japanese with whom he has come in contact.

Another class of foreigner who is apt to mislead people at home on the subject of Japan, but in quite another direction, is he who endeavors to "Japonify" (I did not invent that word) himself at short notice, and without being able to speak the language. He becomes enamoured of the country, and possibly of some one in it, and is rapturously maudlin in telling us all about it.

To such a man Japan is peopled with dear little giggling dolls, living in dear little miniature houses made of "card-board." He eats fairy food out of miniature dishes; hangs the graceful costume of the country on him as if the *kimono* were a towel and he a clothes-horse; he strains the sinews of his legs in squatting on the floor, and tells us that he fears his head would knock a hole in the fragile ceiling if he were to stand upright; and so it would, if he were eight or nine feet high and his head were not softer than the wood-work. He laughs in innocent glee at it all, as he lets the rice fall from his chop-sticks on to the spotless *tatami*, for he is in such a delightful little shallow-minded, light-hearted immoral paradise. He hugs himself in the belief that he is living among laughing children again, and he has no thought for the morrow; for he has not grasped the fact that his companions are bored with it all, but that etiquette and business exigencies oblige them to appear amused at his eccentricities; he does not understand that, if their laugh is genuine, they are laughing at him rather than with him, and that it is he in reality who is the child. Meanwhile his treaty-port guide no doubt is making terms with the landlady of the "card-board" house as to the extent to which it will be safe to run up the bill, and as to how much commission is to be reserved out of that amount for himself.

The above enthusiastic individual, who has solved the Japanese problem to his own satisfaction, will tell us that he has "eaten the lotus," when, in plain English, he has merely become very silly. Such silliness, however, is infectious, and his graphic recital of what he terms his "Adventures in the Land of the Rising Sun" has often had the effect of causing others to visit Japan with the express purpose of endeavoring to emulate him.

A GEISHA ORCHESTRA

POPULAR MISCONCEPTIONS OF JAPAN

Of the changes which are taking place in Japan people hold very varied views, and all that an individual author has a right or is able to do is to give expression to his own personal impressions on the subject, and that with all due respect to the opinions of others. Japan, of course, is being transformed, or, rather, is transforming herself, from her Oriental to our Western methods; but this does not mean that the old Japan has altogether gone, or will ever altogether go. I am aware that in stating this I am taking a diametrically opposite view to that held by most of the acknowledged authorities on the country; but my personal conviction is that although Daimios, Shoguns, and feudalism are things of the past, and although modern education may have shaken the beliefs in ancient superstitions in the minds of the Japanese of to-day, yet his veneration for old traditions is as strong now as it ever was, and he is as purely Japanese in his tastes and convictions. His thoughts—a large proportion of his thoughts, at all events—have turned to things Western, and he has realized that it is essential to the future well-being of his country that he should not only think about but thoroughly understand modern methods. This is not necessarily because he likes them, nor because he considers them to be immeasurably superior to his own, but because he has grasped the fact that to preserve his own country intact he must make the foreigner respect him, and that to effect this purpose he must bring his country into line with Western nations.

There is another very powerful reason, viz., that a Japanese as a rule is by nature and instinct a student, and a very profound student. He is willing and anxious to study any subject, both with regard to its theory and its practice, not necessarily with a view of adopting the policy laid down therein, but in order to put himself in the position of being able to adopt it, either in whole or in part, should he feel that his so doing would be advantageous to himself or to his country.

There are people who hold that the so-called civilization of Japan is only a thin veneer, which will neither bear much investigation nor the test of time; that all that is being done has been due to a vainglorious feeling, brought about more particularly by the success of the late war with China. But such is not the case; for although one may call the Japan of the present day an artificial Japan, in most senses of the word, still the Japanese, who are thorough in everything, are thorough even in their artificiality.

The progress that is being made by the country— if we assume that by "progress" is meant the adoption of Western methods — may be of an artificial nature, but in the long-run it will be found that contact with Europeans will not transform the Japanese into a people with European instincts, but that they will have assimilated and absorbed into their nature so much of our habits as they think advisable.

The local foreign journals are fond of maintaining that the Japanese are merely "aping the foreigner,"

A TOKIO DANCING-GIRL
By the GENROKU-KWAN

POPULAR MISCONCEPTIONS OF JAPAN

but that is hardly the right expression; for to "ape" us would mean to copy us without reason or intelligence. It is true that the Japanese often wear foreign clothes when going about their business and when in contact with a foreigner, either because they find such clothes more practical for certain work; or, if they are in a foreign country, because they know it is the correct thing to do. They use Western buildings and furniture for their modern offices, as they have found it impossible to conduct modern business under Japanese conditions. They learn to speak our language, because this is essential to the new policy of their country. But at home they revert naturally to their methods of life, to their own clothes, and to their own language.

One of the most glaring and oft-repeated of popular fallacies about Japan is that which asserts that everything in that country is little.

Undoubtedly the average stature of the Japanese is somewhat less than that of Europeans and Americans, and their houses and utensils strike us as being somewhat smaller than our own.

Most of the earlier writers noticed and noted that fact, and others took it up until it became a point of honor among foreign scribes never to mention anything Japanese without coupling with it a belittling adjective of some sort. "These delightful little people; their tiny little hands, their polite little manners, their dear little doll's-houses, their funny little waddling walk," and so on, and so on, *ad nauseam*. The general littleness of Japan was as firmly accepted by the foreigner, and as grossly exaggerated as, for instance, are the alleged protruding teeth and red Dundreary whiskers which characterize the Englishman of to-day in French caricature.

There came a time, however, when it was discovered that there were other subjects of interest about the country than the question of dimensions of the people and the things, so the "littleness of Japan" had a holiday for a time, until it was rediscovered as an astounding fact by Sir Edwin Arnold.

In excusing himself for employing the word "little" so often, that talented author urged as an extenuating circumstance that everything in that country was little, except the shrimps, which were colossal, and the sea and the mountains.

This was enough for the purposes of the superficial writer, who, as a rule, and especially if he had never been to Japan in his life, conscientiously applied the wrong end of the telescope to his eye, firmly shut the other, and adapted as the starting-point of his thesis the axiom that everything in Japan was small.

With regard to the theory of the miniature houses in Japan, I should think that the Japanese living in Tokio to-day must have in the way of floor area to their houses a great deal more space per man than has the Londoner in his native city. The Japanese houses look small to us because they do not run into many stories as a rule, and because the rooms are not nearly so high as ours. But if Japanese rooms are two or three feet lower than ours, this is not due

POPULAR MISCONCEPTIONS OF JAPAN

to the average stature of the Japanese people being two or three feet less than that of the Englishman, as the reasoning of certain writers would seem to suggest, but because the normal attitude of a Japanese when inside a room is a sitting one, and he sits on his heels on the floor.

The spirit which tempts people to underrate the size of everything that is Japanese has betrayed more than one foreign writer into describing even the Japanese railways as being built on the microscopic principle, and the trains as being composed of little toy engines and carriages; but when we come down to plain, unvarnished fact we have to admit that the railway gauge of Japan is three feet six inches, which is nearly three inches wider than that of about half the railways in India, in which full-grown Europeans travel comfortably, and that the inhabitants of Ceylon are clamoring to have their gauge reduced to that of the narrow Indian gauge. Thus it is plain that there is nothing much in the above belittling argument.

In olden days there were many excuses for a literature based on what may be called the "comparative dimensions" principle about Japan, for then, except for the temples, the statues of the Daibutzu, the processions, the umbrellas, the wrestlers, and the head-dresses and sashes of the women, most things material were worked out on a smaller scale there than in Europe.

At the present day, however, we are bound to admit that their army, navy, mercantile marine, railway systems, public buildings, educational, political, financial, commercial, and industrial organizations, their asiprations and their doings, must all be accounted large when compared with kindred institutions in the average European country of to-day.

Even the difference in average stature between European and Japanese may be lessened or done away with after a generation or two of youths have been brought up on regular drill, lawn-tennis, baseball, rowing, and bicycling, and nurtured on a diet which has an increasing tendency towards stimulating foods.*

It is, I understand, mainly in the length of leg that the Japanese are deficient from the point of view of our European anthropometrical ideal; and this is said to be due to their native method of sitting down, which tells against leg development. There is a growing tendency to adopt chairs, at all events during the greater portion of the day, in business circles.

Another extremely well-worn fallacy with regard to the Japanese character, but one which fortunately is beginning to wear itself out, is that they are a frivolous people; and, to quote Sir Edwin Arnold once more, "cannot look upon anything seriously." I cannot understand how any student of Japan can draw such a conclusion, although their methods of seriousness may not invariably follow on the lines of ours. The Japanese have, it is true, a keen sense

---

* Meat now is included in the naval diet.

THE JAPANESE BATTLE-SHIP *SHIKISHIMA*
(The most powerful war-ship in the world. Built at the Thames Iron-works)
Drawn by BERNARD F. GRIBBLE

POPULAR MISCONCEPTIONS OF JAPAN

of humor and of the ridiculous, and the spirit of burlesque and caricature is strongly developed in their nature; but in their own particular way I believe that they look on the problems of life at least as seriously as the rest of the world, and that, in their endeavors to probe and solve them satisfactorily, they are often far more persevering and thorough than the people of almost any other nation.

Generally speaking, it may be said that treaty-port pessimism on the one hand, and the superficial and enthusiastic writer on the other, have been responsible for the propagation of most of the many popular fallacies which are generally accepted abroad with regard to the character and doings of the Japanese. But there is a third factor which perhaps may tend to throw the foreigner at home somewhat off the scent in his endeavor to estimate the Japanese of to-day, and that is the impressions he draws from those Japanese whom he sees in his own country.

We must bear in mind that the Japanese who come to England and America from time to time, while being representative of all that is best in the way of progressive Japan from the point of view of the Westernizing of their country, are as a rule picked men, and are nearly always highly educated, even from the foreigner's point of view.

Such men are sent abroad with a set purpose to learn something that the foreigner can teach them, and are consequently chosen on account of their intelligence and aptitude, so that they may absorb as rapidly and effectually as possible the particular knowledge which is to form the subject of their investigations. They are living during the time that they are with us an artificial existence, surrounded by Westerners and Western methods. They have, with that wonderful tact which is one of the most striking traits in the Japanese character, adapted themselves for the time being, and apparently without effort, to our customs and our prejudices. Therefore we must not look on them quite as representing accurately the ordinary Japanese as one finds them in their own country, for the surroundings and conditions are so different as to make comparison impossible.

With all these difficulties, natural and otherwise, in the way of a correct analysis, the visitor has every excuse for drawing inaccurate conclusions with regard to Japan; and it is with just cause that the Japanese complain of the misrepresentation of their country and their methods so frequently made by the foreigner. On the other hand, however, they have been extremely fortunate in the treatment they have received at the hands of many thoroughly competent and experienced writers.

With such exponents as Rein, Mitford, Satow, Brinkley, Hearne, and Chamberlain, to say nothing of earlier authors, it must be admitted that the mythology, history, habits, character, literature, scenery, geography, poetry, science, art, and industries of that country—in fact, all the phases of life which go to make up the old Japan—have been fully and extremely carefully dealt with. In fact, few countries, and certainly no Asiatic countries, have attracted the pen of so many able exponents as has Japan. Unfortunately, however, there have been so many writers who cannot be classed in that category, that the searcher after knowledge is apt to find it a difficult matter to arrive at a determination as to which is which.

CHAPTER II

TRAVELLING AND ACCOMMODATION

NINE people out of ten who go to Japan land in the first instance at Yokohama or Nagasaki, both of which places have been immortalized times out of number by writers of many nations. The opinions concerning those places vary very widely. As a rule, the man who wishes to make a study of the country does not care for the treaty-ports, for he has come to Japan to learn something of the Japanese people and their methods, and the treaty-ports will not help him in any way to obtain that knowledge. The casual visitor, however, usually makes one or other of those places his headquarters, and from time to time runs into the country over the regular routes which are followed by tourists, along all of which he finds accommodation which, if not first-class, is at all events passable, and sufficiently Western to make real discomfort almost an impossibility.

The European hotels in the treaty-ports can only be classed as being good in that they are, as a rule, somewhat better than those which one finds at the ports in other countries east of India, and this is not saying much for them. The best hotels run on

European lines in Japan are found in certain of the big holiday resorts in the interior, such as Miyanoshita and Nikko, and are owned and managed by Japanese. Such good hotels, however, can very easily be numbered on the fingers of one hand. The finest hotel on the European style, as far as appearance is concerned, is the Imperial Hotel at Tokio. It is owned and run by a Japanese company, and subsidized by the Imperial household, but is so eccentrically managed that, while possessing all the features which go to make up first-class accommodation, in the shape of good rooms, good furniture, and good cooking, it lacks just that knowledge on the part of its directors the possession of which would transform it from a rather uncomfortable place of abode into an excellent one.

As a matter of fact, the Imperial Hotel was established by the Japanese for the purpose of affording a place where official and other receptions on European lines could be held, and dinners given as occasion demanded, and the ordinary visitor who puts up there does so at his own risk. He finds plenty of managers and clerks who are civil enough, but he will find that his instructions are ignored, his letters mislaid, and his bell unanswered. He finds plenty of servants, through whom he will have to elbow his way in the passages and public rooms; and should he require to play billiards, he must push them from the table. He finds a splendid dining-room, attended without any system, and a good though limited bill of fare, which, to his dismay, is identical every day.

I think that the transition Japan is exemplified in its very worst phases at the Imperial Hotel in Tokio; for while no doubt everybody about the place is doing what he believes to be the right thing, the people connected with it have not yet learned to understand the foreigner. They have fallen into the error—an error which is not uncommon in Japan just now among people who, having no personal acquaintance with foreign countries, endeavor to assume foreign ways—of believing that, because we are less ceremonious in our manner than they, they should in dealing with us divest their manner of any sort of courtesy. As the Englishman who, without a thorough understanding of Japanese etiquette, endeavors to adopt their style invariably makes himself ridiculous, so those Japanese who mistake our comparatively abrupt ways for a want of courtesy, and endeavor to follow our example, appear to us to be merely boorish and rude.

It is a pity that the Imperial Hotel is not better managed, for it is here that a very large percentage of the foreign visitors acquire their first impressions of Japan and the Japanese after leaving the treaty-ports. Such as it is, however, the Imperial Hotel is almost the only hostelry on "foreign" lines worthy of the name in the immense metropolis of Japan.

The reasons why the casual visitor stays in the treaty-ports, and only visits such places in the interior as may be termed treaty-port haunts, are—firstly, that he cannot make himself understood elsewhere; and, secondly, that he finds a difficulty, which

TRAVELLING AND ACCOMMODATION

is as a rule an insurmountable one, in living for any length of time in Japanese houses and on Japanese food.

Then, again, there is plenty to interest him for a time inside the beaten track without going farther afield. If I were called upon to offer advice to the flying visitor, I should recommend him to stick to such places while he is in the country, unless he happens to be able to travel with some one, other than a professional guide, who knows Japan, speaks the language, and can arrange to supplement the Japanese diet with European necessaries from time to time.

Of life in the treaty-ports, I can only say that as a rule the people who live there dislike doing so; or, at all events, it is their general habit to say that they wish they were not living in Japan.

But, except geographically speaking, they are not in Japan, for the daily routine of the foreigner in the treaty-ports has nothing in common with life elsewhere in that country. It is as accurate a reproduction of life in Europe and America as can be made by so cosmopolitan a community. That the reproduction is not a very faithful one is, under the circumstances, only to be expected, when we take into consideration the conditions of the case. And the most that can be said of it from the point of view of a stranger is that the people have tried to make the conditions of life as bearable as possible, and with considerable success.

I got into terribly hot water when out there for

mentioning in one of my articles that the treaty-port communities were of a mixed nature, and I was told that this statement implied that they contained no gentlefolks. This was not my intention, for among the residents are many of birth, education, and wealth; and as trading communities go, those of the treaty-ports may be described as being of a distinctly creditable standard. But it is difficult to speak of a community drawn from the people of every country of the earth, beginning with Europeans and Americans, and finishing up with Chinamen and mixed Asiatic breeds, and composed of every grade of society, between the professional man and opulent trader on the one hand, and on the other the long-shore loafer and the hanger-on, as otherwise than very mixed.

The visitor who, wearied with a plethora of temples and Daibutzu, and of a fish and rice diet, finds himself back among his own countrymen in the treaty-ports has occasion—an occasion, by the way, of which he rarely avails himself—to thank these residents, from the bottom of his heart, for providing him with the necessaries and luxuries of life, for which he has longed in vain when up-country.

Though, in the treaty-ports or elsewhere, one does not find much in the way of really good hotel accommodation, many of the residents have charming and extremely well-appointed houses; for the man who has command of even a moderate supply of money can surround himself with many, if not most,

TRAVELLING AND ACCOMMODATION

of the minor luxuries which go to make life pleasant. The clubs, too, are very comfortable.

Most of the usual sports are indulged in freely, with the exception of polo, and there are occasional pony races, though these are not up to the standard of those one comes across in many other parts of the Far East. There is no hunting, very little shooting is obtainable now, and good fishing is also scarce, but the yachting and boating are excellent.

As, however, I am not writing a treaty-port guide-book, I do not propose to deal at greater length with the stereotyped resorts of the tourist, my object in this chapter being to point out to the foreigner, in view of the forthcoming opening up of the country, a few of the features of travel and accommodation which go to make up the conditions with which he is likely to meet in travelling about Japan proper, more or less on his own account, at the present day.

It is usually maintained, and very rightly so, that to acquire a knowledge of the Japanese language, even moderately well, is a question of many years of hard study. It is true that one learned author stated that he had accomplished this task after a few months' application, but I cannot for the life of me understand how he did it.

The ordinary person finds the study not only an extremely laborious and lengthy task, but one which, when entered upon seriously, has a faculty for absorbing, or rather blotting out, all other questions for the time being.

But between mastering the Japanese language, in the proper sense of the word, and acquiring a sort of jargon, which can be perfectly well understood for the purposes of the ordinary requirements of life, there is a very wide difference; and there is no reason why any person of ordinary intelligence should not, without any great effort, accomplish the latter feat in two or three months from his arrival.

In undergoing the process, however, he must be prepared to remain out of touch with Europeans, or nearly so, and to run the risk of being considerably bored at times.

The easiest method of acquiring this sort of practical smattering of Japanese is to begin by learning that simple and comparatively modern form of writing known as *Katakana*, which is, in fact, a phonetic alphabet, or syllabary, containing just under fifty characters. This is easily accomplished, and a knowledge of it will enable one to grasp the way in which Japanese words are built up, thereby not only materially assisting the memory with regard to words and phrases, but robbing the Anglo-Japanese phrase-book, which one purchases in the ordinary course, of most of its terrors.

When one glances at such a book for the first time, and learns that the shortest way of saying "I" in respectable Japanese is "Watakushi wa," and that to change that simple pronoun into the plural "we" it is necessary to add two more syllables to the above five, the embryo student may well be excused for standing aghast at the appalling nature of the

TRAVELLING AND ACCOMMODATION

task he had thought of setting himself, and, indeed, for turning tail then and there.

If he masters *Katakana*, however, he will see that a great deal of the length of the words in his book is due to the fact that we are obliged, when trying to convey their sound by Roman characters, to use a great many letters.

The nature of the practical smattering of Japanese that one may learn in the manner above explained will, of course, not be correct, not even at all grammatical; but it will suffice for the requirements of the man who is feeling his way in the interior, and he will improve as he goes. The Japanese are wonderfully quick at grasping a foreigner's meaning, as long as he says his say quietly and does not bully them. If he strings together a number of the substantives which should have a place in his sentence, and applies somewhere or other the required verb, preferably in its root form, and if his pronunciation is within a thousand miles of what it should be, he will be able to make himself understood as a rule. The least sign, however, of blustering or of losing his temper will spoil the situation, and he may rave to any extent he likes to no purpose whatever.

Assuming that a foreigner possessed of the above amount of knowledge of the Japanese language, accompanied by a boy who does not understand English, and armed with his passport, should set out on his travels in the interior, he need have no very serious trouble in finding his way about, as long as he is in no particular hurry.

A great deal has been said to the discredit of the Japanese professional guides, but I do not think, as interpreters go, that they are worse than any others. It is far preferable, however, to do without them, if possible, except within the regular tourist limits, on account of the extreme dislike in which they are held by the hotel people in purely Japanese places. This dislike is due to the fact that when a guide accompanies a party, he usually manages to retain a great portion of the money which would have formed the innkeeper's legitimate profits.

With railway travelling in Japan one has no difficulty, provided always that earthquakes or floods have not damaged or destroyed a portion of the line. There are seldom accidents from any other cause.

People have got into the habit of exaggerating the slowness of Japanese trains. They are, as a matter of fact, a good deal faster than the trains of Norway and similarly mountainous countries, and their mean speed, including goods trains, is about equal to that of the narrow-gauge lines in India.

There are no sleeping-cars on the Japanese lines, and consequently night travelling is not particularly comfortable. And the passenger cannot procure for love or money, anywhere along the line, the proverbial cast-iron sandwich so dear to the travelling Englishman's heart, and, for the matter of that, to his pocket. Excellent beer and excellent lemonade, made in the country, are, however, obtainable wherever railways go; but, as far as solid food is concerned, one must put up with the native luncheon-

THE REMAINS OF THE VILLAGE OF SHIMIDZU AFTER A FLOOD

HAKODATE HARBOR, IN THE HOKKAIDO

boxes, which are sold in pairs, the one containing rice, and the other an assortment of fish, omelette, seaweed, and beans. The whole outfit, including the boxes and the inevitable chopsticks, costs only a penny or two.

On nearly all the lines the tickets bear the names of the departure and arrival stations in Roman characters; and in the stations the practice of printing these names in English is also general.

Baggage is checked on the American system, which is worked very efficiently. With regard to the cost of travelling by railway, one can go first-class for a very long trip for a shilling. This is partly due to the low price per mile, and partly to the low number of miles per hour.

In several of the big provincial towns one finds hotels said to be conducted on the foreign principle, and certain Japanese hotels have a "foreign" side. The European accommodation in such places is, as a rule, terrible. The rooms are dirty, the beds are rickety, the bedclothes are apparently seldom washed, and the tables and chairs are seldom capable of standing on more than two legs at a time.

When I first went to Japan I could not understand how on the "foreign" side of the Japanese hotels the accommodation could be so inferior, when the Japanese portion was kept scrupulously clean. One would naturally think that a people whose houses were so spotless would revolt at having a portion of their premises in a filthy condition. But, as explained to me by the landlord of one of these hybrid establishments, "Foreigners are dirty by nature. They go about their houses in their boots, and consequently they cannot wish to have their rooms kept in proper condition."

This worthy host had never been out of his country, and possibly never to a treaty-port.

When a foreigner arrives at one of these half-and-half hotels, he is invariably pressed to take up his quarters in the European portion of it; firstly, because it is assumed that he will prefer such accommodation; and secondly, because until the people of the house know him they take it for granted that he will disorganize their routine. They expect him to walk about in his boots, to make them put a chair in his room, the legs of which chair will dig holes in the matting; to want all sorts of things which are not at all suited to the accommodation, and to insist on soaping himself in the general bath.

When an individual foreigner is known, however, and it is found that he does not want to indulge in such eccentricities, he is, as a rule, welcomed, or, at all events, tolerated.

There is another reason why the people of the house wish to place the foreigner in the foreign quarter, and that is that they can charge a higher price for accommodating him there.

Many strangers to the country do not understand the method of "tipping," which is an essential feature in Japanese hotel life. This question of giving *chadai*, as it is called, is one of the main difficulties which the verdant foreigner travelling in Japan has

to face. If he has a guide, he will be told by him what to pay in this way; in which case the guide, who handles the money, will probably keep most of it for himself. If he has no guide, he does not know what to give, and offers a modest gratuity, as he would elsewhere, taking as his stand-point that if the bill is low the tip should be proportionately small. This is merely following out in a logical manner our system at home of giving a smaller gratuity in a second-class hotel than we should in a first-class one.

I have heard the *chadai* described as an extortion, and to the newly arrived foreigner it has every appearance of being such.

It was, however, the most just of all systems for a country conducted on the lines of the Japan of the past, though it will hardly adapt itself to the Japan of the future. In these transition days, when European theories, if not methods, are partially understood by the business classes even in the interior, its effect is especially peculiar.

In days gone by the Japanese innkeeper made a small charge for the food he supplied, which charge was presumably assumed to be the cost price, or thereabouts, of the articles supplied. He made no charge for his rooms or for anything else. The guest, on arriving, made a present of money to the house and another to the servants, and the value of these presents was determined by the social rank of the giver and the class of accommodation he looked for. If the sum were large, he was given good rooms and was well looked after, and if it were small his quarters and his attendance were in proportion.

Among Japanese in Japan the system worked well, for the social rank of a guest was at once patent to the host. Now, however, the foreigner comes to these places, and the host knows nothing of his rank, except that he has a notion that all foreigners should be very wealthy. If, therefore, after spending a day and a night in his house, and receiving a bill amounting to say two shillings, the foreigner should offer a gratuity of a shilling, the host, whose profit in the ordinary course would be made out of the *chadai*, may be excused if he feels disappointed and does not wish to see his guest again.

It is now understood by some innkeepers that foreigners look to pay more for their accommodation and less as a gratuity, and they are sometimes charged accordingly. In these transition days, however, the unfortunate foreigner does not know whether he is to be treated as such in his bill, or whether he is expected to make a handsome present on arriving and be presented with a nominal bill for his food when he leaves.

The first time I came face to face with a difficulty of this sort was when, a few months after my arrival, I was spending some days up-country. The bill presented to me on leaving was a ridiculously small one, and, as my knowledge of Japanese was of the crudest, I was glad to apply to a Japanese university student, who spoke a little English, for

TRAVELLING AND ACCOMMODATION

information as to what I should give to the house and to the servants.

"How much did you give them on arriving?" he asked me.

"Nothing," I replied.

"What is your social position?" he queried.

I told him; and he said, "The earnings of people who follow that calling in Japan are not, as a rule, high, but of late years men of good position are connected with newspapers. Are you well off?"

"...," I replied, modestly.

"Then I should give them ...," he said, naming a figure about three times that of my bill. I was rather surprised.

Shortly after the above incident I had occasion to travel up the country with a very rich Japanese gentleman. He had with him one or two friends, and I noticed that wherever he went he and all of us were treated with the greatest respect. The best of rooms and the best of food were forthcoming, and, as he had asked me to accompany him professionally, to advise him on an engineering matter in which he was interested, I was his guest. The first night we put up at one of the best provincial hotels in Japan. It possessed a "foreign" quarter of a sort, and I elected to keep with my friends on the Japanese side. On leaving, I asked one of this gentleman's friends whether it would be the right thing for me to offer some gratuity to the house, and he told me that it would not be accepted if I did.

Some months afterwards I happened to be in the same town, and alone. Remembering my former excellent reception, I went to the same hotel. I was strongly urged by the hotel-keeper to go to the foreign quarters, and on my refusing to do so I was shown into a most comfortless little Japanese room. By this time I had begun to understand in some degree the complicated etiquette of the Japanese hotel. Wrapping up in two separate packets of tissue-paper certain *yen* bills, one being a gift to the house and the other to the servants, and, as is usual when giving a present, scrawling on them the simplest of Japanese hieroglyphics, signifying "common stuff" or "rubbish," I placed them on the floor. The servant took them up and left me. Shortly afterwards the landlady appeared with the usual presents on a tray, and the receipt for the *chadai*.

She said the sum I had given was excessive (it was perhaps rather large, because I felt that on the occasion of my previous visit I had not been allowed to pay for anything). She could not understand, she said, how her servants had shown me into so dirty (*kitanai*) a room (it was extremely clean, as a matter of fact, though small), and that she feared that they had no room worthy of me in the house. As I knew that a few months previously the Mikado and his suite in passing between Tokio and Kioto had engaged this very hotel, the genuine nature of this deprecatory estimate of the available accommodation became apparent. I said that a room similar to the one I had had before would suit me; and when they realized that it was I who had been travelling with Mr. X. (my former friend), I was not only placed in apartments with an area which in a London hotel would have been considered amply large enough to accommodate half a dozen people, but I had extreme difficulty in getting left to myself for a moment during the whole of my sojourn. When at last I thought I had got free from them all for a time, the son of the house brought up a fat Anglo-Japanese dictionary, and seemed anxious to while away a pleasant hour or two in getting me to decipher portions of it for him. Apart from being over-attended, I was extremely comfortable at that place. A couple of days later I received a telegram which necessitated my going right into a portion of the country where there were neither railways nor good quarters. So, being in one of the biggest of Japanese towns, and knowing that for the next few weeks my food, even from a Japanese point of view, would be extremely bad, I instructed the hotel-keeper to lay in for my journey an assortment of tinned provisions and certain other European commodities. This he did. When I applied for my bill before leaving the hotel, I was met with an extremely courteous but very firm refusal. "Mr. X.," they told me, "would be extremely angered if they were to allow me to pay for what I had had."

"But I am not his guest on this occasion, and he is not even here," I explained.

"You were with him before," they replied. "Besides, the liberal *chadai* which you have given more than compensates us for such inferior food and accommodation as you have had."

"But you must let me pay for that case of tinned provisions," I urged.

They regretted that it could not be done; and as I had to catch my train, I left, thinking that when some day I should get back to Tokio I should be able to put matters right with Mr. X. When, however, I did see him, months after, he would not hear of my paying even for the necessaries I had laid in with so lavish a hand for a journey which had nothing whatever to do with him. I mention these personal incidents at this stage, as they serve to illustrate some of the difficulties of a delicate nature which may beset and serve to perplex the unsophisticated traveller in Japan.

On the subject of Japanese accommodation, I had formed, previously to my arrival in the country, an extremely inaccurate idea; and yet, in re-reading some of the descriptions on which I had based my anticipations, I must admit that in words they were often correct.

Of course, I knew that the rooms were low and framed in wood, and floored with spotless matting; that they were fenced in with sliding panels of light woodwork and paper; that they were devoid of furniture as we know it; and that one had to sit on the floor, and to walk about in one's stockinged feet.

All this was true, and it conveyed to my mind

the impression that such accommodation must be comfortless in the extreme. Pictures which I have shown to people of such places since my return almost invariably call forth an expression to the same effect.

Whether I am well advised, or am likely to be successful in endeavoring to elucidate certain features with regard to Japanese accommodation as I found them, I do not know.

Anyhow, I would say that, apart from the question of continually sitting, or rather kneeling, on the floor, the agonies entailed by which process are often much exaggerated, a really good Japanese house, except during the cold weather, is far more comfortable than the *ordinary* so-called "foreign" hotel that one meets with in Japan, away from the treaty-ports and from treaty-port influence.

The first thing one usually does on arriving at a Japanese hotel is to take off one's clothes and have a bath. It is not necessary for the guest to possess a single item of luggage; everything, from night-clothes and day-clothes, for the matter of that, even down to tooth-brushes, is found for him by the house.

The Japanese tooth-brush is merely a stick of soft wood pointed at one end and having the fibre unravelled at the other. When the visitor has made use of this instrument of torture he breaks it in half.

The furniture is spare enough. Mats to sit upon are brought in on one's arrival, and removed when one leaves or goes to bed.

The bed during the daytime is stowed away in a cupboard, and is brought out only when required. Such as it is, I found it very comfortable as a rule, and, in nineteen cases out of twenty, clean. It consists, as most people know, of a few thickly padded oblong quilts, which are placed on the floor. The upper clothes are of a very similar nature, and are applied in a greater or less quantity according to the temperature. The bedding is not washed as often as our sheets, but more often than the blankets in an ordinary European hotel. It is, however, sun-bathed or aired almost daily, and from time to time is unpicked and thoroughly cleaned.

My advice to Europeans travelling in Japan is to take a pair of sheets and a pillow with them. The Japanese pillow is the weakest point in the bed-furniture according to foreign idealists' notions of comfort. It is hard and cylindrical, like a German sausage, about eight inches in diameter, and twelve or fifteen inches long. I do not know the nature of the material used in making up the interior of an ordinary pillow, but on one occasion, when I complained to a landlady that it was rather like a brick, she triumphantly brought me one which she seemed very proud of, and which she told me was stuffed with tea. When I explain that this pillow seemed luxurious and downy in comparison with those I had previously tried, the solid consistency of the ordinary Japanese pillow can be imagined.

I feel that in treating this subject I should tell once more the harrowing tale of how the Japanese

TRAVELLING AND ACCOMMODATION

women torture themselves by sleeping with their heads on blocks of wood, for that is the theory which is usually accepted in Europe and America.

However, it is only true in a figurative sense. To describe it accurately, one must say that they sleep with their necks resting on a pillow, a portion of which is made of wood. But the wooden portion does not touch them, as above it is fixed a padded roll of a softer consistency, and presumably made on the same lines as the pillows first described; but it is only three inches in diameter by six or eight inches long. Outside this roll paper is wound and changed as often as required. In many parts of the country these are the only pillows available for either sex; and I can only say that, as far as I am concerned, I have slept more comfortably with my neck on the bar of a chair.

My impression is that the pillow I first described —that made on the sausage principle—is a comparatively modern institution, and represents the only sign of transition from native towards Western methods that is to be found in Japanese bedding.

No ablutions, or any other functions of the toilet except hair-dressing, which is done by professional hands, are carried on in one's room. In certain passages water-stands are placed with metal basins for washing one's hands and face. These are usually half in the open air and half under cover. They do not, however, play an important part in the ablutions of the Japanese; for the bath is the real thing, and is indulged in so frequently—in the summer sometimes three or four times a day—that very little supplementary washing is needed.

Now I do not disguise from myself that, owing to the extraordinary accounts I had read as to what constituted a Japanese bath, I was in a "blue funk" on the subject when for the first time I left the beaten track, with the firm conviction that I must face the terrible alternative of going unwashed for a month, or of losing forever my self-respect.

I had been told that when a foreigner indulged in a bath in such places it was an occasion for all the population to come out and see him do it; that the Japanese regarded the spectacle as a free show, in which the foreign victim played the dual part of a clown and a "freak" from Barnum's.

I had been told that everybody bathed together indiscriminately, and that the only sign that the Japanese had given of their appreciation of Western notions of modesty had taken the form of fencing off the gentlemen's portion of the bath from that of the ladies' by the solid protection afforded by a bamboo rod simply floating on the water.

Well, some of this is true and some is not, as is usually the case with regard to accepted notions of Japanese methods.

As a matter of fact, in such Japanese hotels as are frequently visited by foreigners, there is usually bath accommodation of a sort where the European can disport himself in privacy. It may only be a wooden tub, but he will be able to have it in a room or an out-house by himself. In such hotels

TRAVELLING AND ACCOMMODATION

as are visited by foreigners only occasionally, the people of the house and the Japanese guests will, as a rule, endeavor, at great inconvenience to themselves, to arrange matters so that while the stranger is in the bath-room he has it to himself. It is only in the hotels away from the ordinary tourist track that the foreign visitor need run any risk of finding ladies and gentlemen strolling in while he is in the middle of his bathing operations. His companions of the bath, however, have not come to see him, but have entered a public room to do what he is doing; and unless he is eccentric in his behavior they will not pay any attention to him, but merely take their clothes off and commence their ablutions. If, however, the outraged foreigner should become pale with anger, or scarlet with shame, or should exhibit an ungentlemanly curiosity about his neighbors, his behavior will be resented, and may cause him to be the object of ridicule.

Let him then, if he should find himself in that predicament, devote all his energies to smothering his feelings, whether of indignation, shame, or curiosity. Let him imagine, if he can, that there are no people within miles of him, or that he is sitting in an ordinary smoking or reading room in a European hotel; and, above all, let him take everything he sees for granted, and not appear surprised or shocked.

The Japanese bath in its ordinary form is a rectangular structure made mostly of wood, and is usually let in so that its top is more or less flush with the floor. The water is let in cold through a bamboo tube, and is heated in the bath by a fire underneath or on one side of it. In measure as it becomes too hot, more cold water is admitted through the supply-pipe. No doubt the Japanese habitually take their baths very warm, but the harrowing accounts of their entering them at a temperature which would boil a European must be classed as figurative rather than accurate statements. For leprosy, which the Japanese consider to be under certain conditions a curable disease, and for certain disorders of the skin, naturally medicated springs are utilized for baths, and at a very high temperature. But the ordinary hotel bath, though possibly somewhat warmer than our baths, is seldom too hot for a European to use without serious discomfort. In cases where accommodation is poor, the bath consists merely of a wooden tub of tolerably large dimensions, sufficiently high to enable one when sitting down to have the water up to one's chin.

The better rectangular structures, previously described, vary in size from about four feet long by three feet wide, up to ten or twelve feet long by six or eight feet wide in some of the hotels.

The water is seldom changed more than once or twice a day, except in places where the natural hot springs of the country are available, in which case the water renews itself automatically and continually. Under ordinary conditions, therefore, from a score to a hundred people might bathe practically in the same limited amount of water which a bath of given dimensions will hold. Now, at first sight this would

TRAVELLING AND ACCOMMODATION

strike the Englishman as a very dirty arrangement, and so it would be if the Japanese treated the bath as we do—that is to say, as a place to wash in—but he does not. He gets into his bath for the purpose of raising the temperature of his body after he has been thoroughly washed all over, and on leaving it he is immediately washed all over again, before he puts his clothes on.

The ordinary routine is as follows, and in explaining it I am assuming that the foreign bather has adopted the Japanese costume for the time being, as it is impossible to live comfortably in a Japanese house in any but the native garb.

On entering the bath-room, which may have one or more native guests of either sex in it at the time, he divests himself of his clothes, and places them on a tray or shelf provided for the purpose. The bath attendant provides him with a couple of buckets of water, one hot, one rather cold, and while sitting on a low stool on the slightly inclined floor the patient lathers himself all over with soap and water. The attendant will assist him with such portions of his body as may be difficult to get at, and if not pressed for work with other customers will carry out the whole process for him. The buckets of water are constantly renewed, and after being soused with clean water to wash the soap off, and thumped between the shoulder-blades and in the back of the neck, he gets into the bath.

Even if the bath is unoccupied when he enters it, he cannot expect in a busy Japanese hotel that it will remain so; and while, as I have above explained, the Japanese will always do their best to avoid bathing at the same time as a foreigner, it is hardly to be expected that when they are ready to get into the bath they will stand shivering until the foreigner has finished. Thus the foreigner who has temporarily adopted the Japanese style of living must not be disconcerted if, when sitting in his bath, one, or two, or three ladies should come and sit down beside him. If they do not know him, they will take no notice of him; but if one of them happens to be his landlady, or some one who has previously conversed with him in the hotel, she may address some commonplace remark to him on the heat of the water, or any other topic; but it will all be done so much as a matter of course that the most prurient-minded member of a modern vigilance committee would find it a difficult matter to twist the situation into anything suggestive of vulgarity, or of a want of modesty. An eccentric situation, if you will, from our point of view, but not an indecent one from theirs. The man who wishes to keep clean in Japan must not leave the beaten tourist track, unless he is prepared to undergo over and over again the above ordeal; and for the European lady it is obvious that the situation would be even more trying.

Except in quite small villages the foreigner need not patronize the public baths, for he will find a bath on the lines above described in his hotel; but even when he does, he need not excite attention or curiosity among the natives unless his eccentric behavior occasions it.

The vexed question as to how one should deal with Japanese food is a very favorite theme with authors, and it is treated in a very great variety of manners. I read in a recent book how a European married a charming Japanese lady, and soon tired of her because she would insist on eating pork cooked in rancid oil. Where she acquired the habit did not transpire; but the fact remains that the Japanese do not eat pork as a native dish at all, and do not use oil of any sort in their cooking. Possibly the author was confounding Japan with China or Spain. The best authorities agree generally that Japanese food is usually extremely clean, and is served artistically and most delicately; that some of it is rather eatable, but that most is extremely nasty to the taste; and I think that, with hardly one exception, they maintain that a European cannot live on it satisfactorily for any length of time.

I quote the above opinion because I believe it to be the right one to go upon, in spite of the fact that it does not in the least accord with my personal experience. There is no doubt, however, that ninety-nine Englishmen out of a hundred, after reading the above opinion and then my own, would, if they were to go to Japan and try the experiment for themselves, come to the conclusion that most of what I am about to say would not coincide with their own experiences.

It is possible that the nature of my training in the art of relishing Japanese food has unfitted me for looking at it from the point of view of the foreigner; for, after a very lengthy and severe illness, I was brought back to life, or at all events to health, upon it as my staple, and for a long time my only solid diet.

During the long period of convalescence which followed my illness, I acquired naturally and without effort the handling of chopsticks, which I was encouraged to use, I am told, partly because they were lighter than a spoon and fork, and could be manipulated by one hand, and partly because the doctors wished me to have only very little food at a time, and to make the process of disposing of it as lengthy as possible.

Thus it was that by the time I was well again I had acquired a liking for Japanese food, and could manipulate it without difficulty in the native manner.

On several occasions after this, when right away in the interior, I had occasion to live for weeks at a time on this diet, often of a very bad quality, and I can only say that while I often wished I could indulge in a beefsteak and bread, it was no sort of an effort to me to do without these luxuries, and I found that the diet agreed with me in every way.

I often think that the real reason why the foreigner dislikes Japanese food is not so much on account of its ingredients as because of the difficulty he has in getting it comfortably. I think that the guests at a Mansion House banquet would not do justice to

TRAVELLING AND ACCOMMODATION

the viands, however choice they might be, if five minutes after they had sat down they were all suffering from pins-and-needles, cramp or numbness in their lower extremities, and if they found that three-quarters of their food was slipping from their fork every time they raised it to their lips. They would get bored at their constant failures, and at their uncomfortable position, and would leave the table hungry. This is why we are told that it is impossible for Europeans to satisfy their natural appetite on a Japanese diet. For eating Japanese food in the native manner, until one can use the chopsticks easily, is something like trying to help one's self to soup with a fork; and the attitude one assumes on the floor of a Japanese house does not lend itself to extreme comfort from our point of view for more than a minute or two at a time.

In briefly sketching a few of the phases connected with travel and accommodation in Japan at the present day, my object has been to show that while we hear so much of the modern progress of the Japanese, a progress which in a book of this sort I must necessarily emphasize, we must not run away with the supposition that Japan proper is at all like a Western country, or that the people in it are at all like Western people. My personal impression is that they will not become so within measurable time; for, while it may answer their purpose to master our sciences and our methods, they will merely apply them to their style of life, and not necessarily adopt our style. They require modern soldiers and sailors and business men, and ships and railways and telegraphs and machinery, to enable them to keep pace with their foreign competitors and to keep their country for themselves. But all these things can be adopted without radically changing the methods of conducting their homes, that is to say, of their inner life. At all events, we may take it that domestic Japan will be the last feature in that country to give way to what we are pleased to term "civilization."

No doubt, when the whole country has been thrown open to the foreigner, foreign influence may make itself felt in domestic matters to a degree which has hitherto been impossible, owing to the restrictions entailed by the treaty-port system, but it is too early to indulge in conjectures on that subject. At the present day one can travel throughout the greater portion of Japan, that portion which is seldom visited by the tourist, without seeing much to indicate the great progress that has been made at the ports and the great political, industrial, and trading centres.

Away from these one sees occasionally a building which does not look quite Japanese in style, the inevitable telegraph wire, the railway track, and the policemen in European dress. In the shops we find side by side with the simple and artistic utensils of the Japanese household modern clocks of vulgar design and cheap and ugly oil-lamps; the beautiful, though cumbersome, Japanese umbrella is being replaced by the utilitarian European "gamp" in its

TRAVELLING AND ACCOMMODATION

most unprepossessing form; the round felt hat is *en évidence* now as a national head-gear; and one comes across an odd-looking bicycle or two, tinned provisions, matches, beer, and lemonade, even in the villages.

It is true that in some of the large cities certain wealthy men have added foreign rooms to their houses, but this has not been for the purpose of living in them. It merely means that they have been built to be used on occasion, possibly for receiving foreigners, or for entertaining Japanese friends in a European style.

There is, as previously explained, a slight tendency on the part of the Japanese to modify and strengthen their diet, which may be due to change in the physical education of the Japanese of to-day, and to the spread of the knowledge of Western medical and hygienic sciences; but this feature has not yet developed to any marked degree away from the great centres. Still, such as it is, it forms the most distinct feature of change in the domestic routine of the country up to the present time.

CHAPTER III

THE STANDING OF THE FOREIGNER

WE are asked to accept as a fact beyond dispute or question that the Japanese are without gratitude to the foreigner for the great good he has wrought in modernizing their country. We are told that it is the foreigner who has made the New Japan, and it is impressed upon us that in so doing he has conferred an inestimable blessing on the Japanese nation.

Certain it is that modern progress in Japan could not have arrived at its present state unless the foreigner's aid had been called in on every conceivable modern subject, and unless the foreigner had given that aid unsparingly and with great skill. Certain it is that without the possession of a knowledge of Western methods the Japanese nation would be declining in power, or perhaps might years ago have been absorbed by Russia or some other State. Therefore it may be taken that the benefits so lavishly bestowed by the foreigner have been of a real and tangible nature.

But in justice we must admit—firstly, that the foreigner, in carrying out his work, has had to do with extremely apt and eager pupils; and, secondly, that the Japanese have been willing to pay for any foreign advice they have applied for.

In many countries we are obliged to force our methods on the natives if we wish to have them adopted, but in Japan this has never been necessary, as far as education is concerned, since the Americans obliged the Japanese Government to open certain treaty-ports to the foreigner in 1854.

Speaking generally, and excluding Legation and Consular officials, there are four classes of foreigners in Japan, and the benefits conferred on the Japanese by them are of a varied nature.

1st. The business foreigners. These may justly claim to have built up the international trade of the country.
2d. The missionaries. These may justly claim to have taught English to many of the Japanese.
3d. The passing visitors. These may justly claim to have spent a certain amount of money in the country.
4th. The few technical advisers and others who, for one reason or another, live among the Japanese. These may justly claim to have done far more than all the rest of the foreigners in bringing about the enlightened Japan of the present day.

One of the principal grievances of the business foreigner is that now that the Japanese are capable of carrying on much of their international trade without his assistance they are passing him over; and it is precisely the business man who is the most bitter in his cry about the ingratitude of the Japanese. However, he, at all events, ought to have the consolation of knowing that in the past he has been amply compensated in hard cash for his enterprise. It would be straining a point to assume that the motives of the foreign trader in establishing himself in Japan were purely of a philanthropic nature: nor would it be natural or right that such should have been the case. Therefore one cannot see how, even if the Japanese of to-day are not such profitable customers as in times gone by, the business foreigners can have any very just claim against them for want of consideration on this particular count. They have, however, every reason to complain of the lines on which many of the Japanese conduct their foreign business.

The fact of the matter is that the various foreign governments have not studied the interests of, or backed up, their business compatriots in Japan; and under these circumstances it is hardly fair for us to lay all the blame on the Japanese if they have taken advantage of this fact.

International gratitude of any sort is a very doubtful quantity, and not to be relied upon at the best of times; and international business gratitude is practically non-existent, unless there is a solid business moral at the bottom of it, and then it is no longer a question of gratitude, but of interest.

It is hard to understand why we should claim so much business gratitude from the Japanese, for it would certainly never enter our heads to expect such a quality in the French or Germans, or anybody else with whom we deal; and if we are to judge by the Continental press, it will be seen that the people of those nations do not consider that English people are overburdened with this ideal virtue.

THE STANDING OF THE FOREIGNER

From the missionary point of view, the Japanese no doubt display their ingratitude by accepting a free education and refusing to adopt Christianity. But unfortunately the missionaries have not yet come to an agreement between themselves as to the lines on which Christianity should be preached, and consequently a Japanese, if he were to feel in-inclined to adopt Christianity, may be excused if he does not know which of the many conflicting sections of that faith he ought to follow.

The tourists, on their part, complain of Japanese ingratitude when they find that after treating their guide very liberally he has been taking a commission on everything that they have been purchasing, and otherwise abusing their confidence. No doubt such people fully expected to come across primitive, unsophisticated man in the shape of a Japanese treaty-port guide. On finding their guides to be no more honest than is usual with the tourist guides in highly civilized countries nearer home, the visitor becomes unjustly indignant with Japanese methods when he reflects that he could have arranged to have been robbed in a similar and more extensive manner without going half-way round the world.

With regard to the position of foreign advisers, it is often alleged, though not as a rule by the advisers themselves, that the Japanese treat them very unfairly. Unless, however, we are to assume that the discharging of their instructors as soon as they feel that their own knowledge is sufficient to enable them to get along without them constitutes a sign of ingratitude, we cannot call the Japanese absolutely ungrateful.

The practice of discharging the foreigner as soon as possible has been invariably adopted in Japan; and, since the war with China, this policy has been much more marked than was the case previously. This is natural enough, as the Japanese no doubt became unduly elated at their successes, and have been wont to overrate, to some extent, their power of getting along unaided. But undue elation and self-confidence follow as a matter of course with any nation which has just carried out a successful war; and certain it is that the behavior of the Japanese, after their marvellous achievement in this way, would compare favorably with what might be expected in the case of any other nation in the world under similar conditions.

After all is said and done, we cannot get away from the fact that we, in England and elsewhere, are in the habit of dispensing with our instructors, native or foreign, as soon as they have finished instructing us. Our boys do not remain with their army and navy crammers after they have passed their examinations; and comparatively few of us ever set eyes on our teachers again after we have completed our education. Yet we should not expect to be charged with ingratitude on that account.

If we, in England, drop out of touch with our former instructors naturally, and as a matter of course, and when our methods of life are identical with theirs, it is only to be expected that when

THE STANDING OF THE FOREIGNER

the business contact is over between the Japanese pupil and the foreign instructor, however kindly a feeling may exist between them, they should gradually but surely fall apart, for their ways of living do not run on similar lines. I am bound to say that in conversation with many Japanese, who had passed through the hands of various foreign instructors during the course of their education, I have found that they invariably spoke with respect, and sometimes with affection, of their former teachers.

That the Japanese have been well served by their advisers and instructors in nearly every branch of foreign learning is expressing the matter in unduly mild terms. To one whose business it is to study the modern developments that have taken place in that country, and to note the solid foundation on which the modern knowledge of the Japanese has taken root, the question as to which was the greater factor in the creation of the New Japan —the aptitude of the pupil or the conscientiously applied skill of the instructor — must continually occur to him. And he will find it difficult to answer.

The foreigners who are still retained in this capacity are mostly English, with a few Americans and Germans, and a Frenchman or two.

Speaking generally, England may claim to have taken the largest part in organizing the navy, finance, communications, mining, and industrial work; Germany devoted herself mostly to the army, medicine, and several scientific subjects. America has had a hand in almost all departments, more particularly with regard to educational and industrial matters; and to France belongs the chief credit of having given the preliminary advice which led to the formation of the existing legal code, and of organizing on modern lines the Yokosuka dock-yard, which until now has been considered the leading naval depot of the country. An interesting feature about Yokosuka is that centuries ago it was the place of residence of the first foreign adviser whom the Japanese ever employed, one "Will" Adams, an Englishman, who in 1600 was cast ashore in a storm while piloting a Dutch fleet. If the affection of the Japanese for their foreign advisers were as strong to-day as it was then, one could not accuse them of any want of appreciation. For their attachment to Mr. Adams was so marked that they would not let him return home to his wife and family, but retained him in the mixed capacity of shipbuilder-in-chief and agent for the reception of foreigners, found him a Japanese wife, treated him with every honor, and raised a monument to his memory over his grave, which the guide-books tell us is "revered to this day."

The position of the foreign advisers who still remain in the service of the Japanese, though modified, is by no means less important than it was. In times gone by, and not so very long ago, they were the active responsible directors. They had the organizing and practical working out of their various subjects, and carried on the management of their respective departments.

THE STANDING OF THE FOREIGNER

The Japanese, with their growing knowledge, and their anxiety to take the reins into their own hands, have now assumed the active direction of their own affairs in almost every branch of their modern organizations. Thus the foreign employé is no longer on the executive staff, but is retained purely as a consultant. Often, no doubt, it would be better for the Japanese if they would allow the foreigner more direct control than he has, for their own knowledge on all subjects cannot yet have developed entirely. But it was merely a question of time as to when this change should come, and if the Japanese have somewhat anticipated the ideal moment, they have at all events retained a certain, though limited, number of their foreign employés ready to their hand as advisers in case of need.

And here again the Japanese have shown wonderful tact in their choice of those whom they have retained, for while, doubtless, they have allowed many good men to leave the country, for one reason or another, they have realized that it was necessary to make it worth the while of equally efficient experts to remain with them.

The number has dwindled down, it is true, very materially, but it is possible that it has just now reached its lowest ebb for some time to come, as there is, I believe, a slight tendency to engage a few new men, at all events, in temporary capacities.

The relations between the Japanese and their foreign advisers, if not of an effusive nature, are often cordial and sympathetic, and while there must arise, between people belonging to nations so widely different in their traditions and methods, questions and situations which both cannot look at from a similar stand-point, their attitude towards each other is, generally speaking, one of mutual respect.

The irony of the foreign advisers' position lies in the fact that, while many of them are men with a world-wide reputation, whose advice in their own or in most other countries would not only command respect but would bear a high market value, and while they are paid by the Japanese to advise them, their advice is very often ignored. The fact of the matter is that the New Japan which, when in its infancy, left herself in the hands of the foreigner, is anxious, now that the people of the country are progressing in modern accomplishments, to feel that she is acting on her own initiative, even when mistakes are made by so doing, and when she has to suffer in consequence.

The state of the modern development of the country may be said to have reached that awkward age at which the youth is anxious to shake off preceptorial control, and is perhaps a little ashamed of acknowledging that, here and there, there are a few remaining leading-strings which it will not be politic to detach altogether just yet. Thus the Japanese keep their foreign advisers somewhat in the background; and it is perhaps for this reason that we hear little or nothing about this small body of highly educated and interesting men who have done and are doing so much for that country.

THE STANDING OF THE FOREIGNER

The casual visitor, the casual book-writer, haunts the treaty-ports; and, as he finds that the treaty-port residents do not mix in any way with the Japanese, and never have, he is apt to draw the conclusion, when he goes to Tokio and sees some of the big modern institutions there, that the Japanese have "done it all by themselves," and he naturally wonders how they managed to do it. Consequently he will very possibly draw an exaggerated estimate of their capabilities.

Possibly such a man will hardly make the acquaintance of any of the foreign employés who live there, for the latter have neither an interest in business matters nor any particular wish to cultivate the society of strangers; and, living away from the coast, they are not so often pestered by the letter-of-introduction fiend, as is the case with their long-suffering compatriots within the concession limits.

The casual visitor, if he happens to come in contact with the Japanese of a respectable class, nearly always comes away with the idea, not only that they are an extremely agreeable, intelligent, and enlightened people, which is true enough, but that he has made a favorable impression on them, which is often not the case. This is due to two reasons—the conduct of such Japanese will usually be courteous and very modern, and they will nearly always be glad to have an opportunity of conversing with a newly arrived foreigner. The visitor in Tokio, with an introduction or two to Japanese business people, will have no difficulty whatever in finding plenty of educated Japanese men ready to take him about and to put themselves to no end of trouble for him. But this is not necessarily due to friendship, but rather to an intelligent curiosity.

The Japanese are often glad to meet a new-comer, either to practise talking English with him, or to learn his ideas, so that they can compare his views with those of the resident foreigner. The newcomer is apt to imagine that he has made unusual progress, and cannot understand how it is that the local foreigner persists in telling him that the Japanese are difficult people to get on with, and that to obtain an insight into their character and feelings would mean the solving of one of the most complicated problems in the world. He considers that he has found it all out at the end of a week; for he has mistaken a passing interest, created by curiosity in a passing man, for a frank and sudden friendship for which there would really be no *raison d'être*. He will find that, if he remains in the country for any length of time, unless he can manage to sustain that feeling of curiosity about his personality in the mind of his Japanese acquaintance, the friendship so suddenly born will as suddenly die.

I do not mean to suggest by the above that *bona fide* friendships do not exist between individual Japanese and individual foreigners; but that the general bearing of the Japanese is such as to impress the newly arrived foreigner with the fallacious notion that he has rapidly formed a number of friends.

THE STANDING OF THE FOREIGNER

The Japanese are not fond of foreigners in the abstract, and I do not know why one should expect them to be so. In their heart of hearts very few people in any country are fond of foreigners as a class. Foreigners all over the world are tolerated with a greater or less degree of cordiality according to the temperament of the natives of the country of their adoption, and according to the amount of advantage their presence may occasion to that country. In Europe we have recognized that, in these modern days of international intercourse, the foreigner is a necessity, perhaps a necessary evil, but a necessity; and he is treated with a show of cordiality which in many individual cases ripens into a real friendship. Such is the case in Japan, and we have no right to expect more.

There are many real and solid friendships existing between individual foreigners and individual Japanese; but in the first flush of the manhood of the New Japan, and with their successful war in the immediate background, the general feeling of the Japanese just now is undoubtedly that the foreigner will soon be a useless person. Thus, among the many things which they have borrowed and adapted from the foreigner, and one which has met with the greatest popularity, is the cheap war-cry of "Japan for the Japanese." To a nation which is professing to run on the lines of a broad policy, and which is endeavoring to cultivate a big mercantile marine, and to become an international carrying power, the fallacy of such a doctrine should be apparent, and no doubt will become so in course of time.

Meanwhile the position of the foreigner in Japan is a strange one. The presence of the permanent business resident foreigner is resented, the missionaries are treated with indifference, and the globetrotter with curiosity. Apart from the foreign diplomatic officials, whose relations with the Japanese are purely formal, the advisers and the few business men who live away from the treaty-ports, who mix with the Japanese, and treat them on a basis of equality, are, as a rule, the only foreigners who can be said to command any real respect just now.

In justice to the Japanese we must remember that it was only the most binding of laws, the contravention of which often entailed capital punishment, that restrained this energetic people from acquiring a knowledge of the outer world centuries ago. When, therefore, the treaty-ports were opened and foreigners began to pour into them, it was in the natural order of things that the Japanese should rush to the new-comers for instruction and advice. It did not matter much what sort of a foreigner the man applied to might be—a German stoker, an English billiard marker, or an American shoe-black—it was certain that he would be able to tell the Japanese something that they did not know before. Consequently in those days the foreigner, on account of his wonderful knowledge on a variety of subjects with which the Japanese were unacquainted, was perhaps an unduly exalted personage in their then uneducated eyes. Now, however, he must suffer from the reaction due to the exaggerated estimate which the Japanese formed of his knowledge in those early days. The tendency at the present day is undoubtedly to unduly discredit his capacity because the Japanese, now that they have acquired a certain amount of Western knowledge themselves, are able to appreciate the fact that, among the people to whom they were wont to apply for advice, were some who were not perhaps either very highly educated or very competent.

Of course this present feeling is quite as unreasonably pessimistic as the former was unreasonably optimistic; for the treaty-port communities, as international trading communities go, are certainly up to the quality that one might expect with regard to re-respectability and business integrity; and among the residents there are many highly educated and honorable men who would do credit to any community in the world. Of course there are many who do not come up to that standard, as all sorts and conditions of men drift out to those places. A town which has always a shifting population of the sailors of all nations, and other people of noisy habits and a low class, is hardly likely to offer a good impression of the foreigner to the Japanese, who naturally base their estimate of foreigners rather on the noisy and aggressive than on the quiet and respectable element.

To bring home the impression which is held by the Japanese of the foreigner, I quote below from the *Japan Mail* the translation of one of Count Okuma's speeches on the subject:

"Comparing Europeans and Japanese, I do not think that the Europeans then (thirty years ago) in Japan were a particularly high class of persons; nor do I think that those here now are particularly high class. On the whole, I think they would not have been reckoned higher than middle-class in Europe. Among diplomatic officials there may have been men of high standing, but the general run of merchants were of the middle and lower classes. Middle and lower classes though they did belong to, however, when we compare them with the Japanese of the time, how great was the difference in the degree of their civilization. The foreigners living in Yokohama, Nagasaki, and so forth, seemed to know everything, and were many degrees superior to the Japanese. Their ideas were so large that the Japanese were quite astounded. I was a student at the time, and I remember that on one occasion, thinking that a certain foreigner was a wonderful scholar, I went to ask him a question, but when I look back now I recognize that he was not equal even to a Japanese middle-school graduate. Still I was surprised at the explanations I received from him."

Count Okuma is not a man who speaks either lightly or uselessly, and is certainly one of the greatest, if not the greatest, statesman in Japan. His expressions with regard to the foreigner, above quoted, may be taken as affording a representative and moderate opinion as held by the better-class Japanese of to-day, and I quote them as such. There still remain fiery orators who advocate the suppression of all foreigners from time to time, but the Japanese press as a rule ridicule and condemn the speeches of such gentlemen.

It is only when one knows a Japanese extremely well that he will state his real opinion of the for-

COUNT OKUMA

Photographed by OGAWA

THE STANDING OF THE FOREIGNER

eigner, and when he does it is often both sweeping and uncomplimentary. In conversation with a Japanese gentleman who is well known both in Japan and in Europe, on the question of the anti-foreign feeling, he remarked that the Englishman in England was of quite a different stamp from the Englishman in Japan; as the latter was totally unable to distinguish the difference between a Japanese gentleman and a coolie, with the result that "the local foreigners treated all Japanese like rikisha boys."

This may hold good with regard to certain local foreigners and tourists, but it is not at all justified in the case of many of the residents.

I feel that I am plagiarizing everybody who has written on the subject of Japan when I say that the term "Ketojin" or "hairy barbarian" is the contemptuous method employed by the Japanese to designate the foreigner. The freedom, however, with which this expression is employed by the Japanese of the present day, who usually take it for granted that no foreigner understands anything of their language, makes it very obvious that the spirit of contempt which centuries ago gave birth to this opprobrious title still holds good to a great extent.

After all, the people of most nations have methods of designating the people of others by means of epithets which are neither less forcible nor in better taste, and, while sometimes the employment of such terms may add to the gayety, it seldom affects detrimentally the relations of the nation in question.

CHAPTER IV

PRESENT DAY EDUCATION

THE earliest authenticated educational code in Japan was promulgated during the first years of the eighth century in the reign of the Emperor Mombu.

As educational codes go, it was of course primitive enough, providing as it did merely for a certain amount of instruction for Court officials. But all things must have a beginning, and the example afforded by this particular code, with its narrow scope, was soon followed and improved upon. The educational circle soon after expanded until it embraced the *samurai*, who, as a class, can perhaps best be described as corresponding to something between the knights and the squires who were retained in the service of our barons in the days of feudalism in England.

At that time the complete *samurai* was expected to be proficient in etiquette, horsemanship, archery, music, reading, writing, and arithmetic; that is to say, he had to attain seven accomplishments, the last four of which were not considered at all necessary to his British equivalent at the period in question.

PRESENT DAY EDUCATION

However, it was not until the commencement of the Meiji era, a little over thirty years ago, when the Shogunate came to an end, that education of a solid description spread downward in any marked degree below the official classes.

Kioto, the ancient capital of Japan, may be said to have been the birthplace of the first properly organized attempt at a general system of academical instruction, and this event took place in 1868, when an Educational Board was started in that city.

The schools which had been authorized during the régime of the Tokugawa Shogunate, and had been run in an unsystematic manner, were reconstituted, and others were opened on somewhat new lines; and eventually the whole system was brought under the direct control of the Government Department of Education established in 1871.

This date may be fixed as the starting-point of education in Japan on modern or Western lines, for at this period commissioners were despatched by the Government to the various civilized countries to report as to the best means of bringing Japan into educational line with the most advanced of foreign nations.

The immediate result of this was the foundation of a code which, in substance and in fact, was practically identical with that in force in the United States at the time, and I believe I am right in stating that the first foreign adviser to the Japanese Government on educational matters was an American, Mr. David Murray.

The Mikado's edict as to the aims of the educational system, rendered freely in English, was as follows:

"All knowledge, from that essential for ordinary requirements, to the higher accomplishments necessary to prepare officers, landowners, merchants, artists, physicians, etc., for their respective callings, is acquired by learning. It is intended that henceforth education shall be so diffused that there may not be a village with an ignorant family, nor a family with an ignorant member."

Such a programme was ambitious enough in all conscience, and would seem to indicate an ideal which has not up till now been attained in any known country; but, ambitious as it was, the Japanese have never lost sight of it, and probably never will, until they have reached as near to its accomplishment as can ever be attained when one is striving after the impossible.

Education and the educational code encountered many vicissitudes, and underwent constant revision; but, however chaotic its condition, its progress was always in the right direction; the next notable step being the founding of the Imperial University of Tokio in 1877, out of a nucleus formed of various then existing schools.

By that time many foreign professors had been imported from England, America, Germany, and France, and the higher branches of learning, such as law, medicine, science, and art, were in full swing.

Passing to more recent times, I think in 1882 or 1883, the general system of education which prevails to-day was inaugurated by Viscount Mori Arinori,

VISCOUNT YOZO YAMAO
Minister of Education during the early struggles of the modern educational movement

PRESENT DAY EDUCATION

a most energetic and enlightened diplomatist, who, coming fresh from the go-ahead influences of Washington, where he had acted as Japanese Minister, was appointed Minister of Education in his own country.

He held this position until he was assassinated in 1889, and during his term of office worked wonders in the way of forwarding the education of his fellow-countrymen. He advocated strongly the policy of a compulsory and free education for all, general conscription, and an enforced service under Government by the graduates for a given number of years after leaving college; the nature of such service to be determined by the particular branch of technical knowledge which an individual student had attained. In getting these strong precepts carried out he was partially successful.

Of modern education, from its early days until comparatively recent times, a writer in the *Kokumin-no-Tomo* gives the following figures as to the total roll-call of students and graduates in the various educational establishments throughout the country:

1873	1,180,000
1879	2,210,000
1885	3,180,000
1891	3,630,000

Personally I think these figures are a little optimistic; and in any case the accuracy of statistics in those days was not altogether to be depended on.

Government tables, published in November, 1897,

show the following results since years above referred to:

1892	3,698,536
1893	3,897,401
1894	4,091,110
1895	4,290,487

During the same period the increase in the number of schools of all sorts was proportionate, and as follows:

1892	25,375
1893	25,594
1894	25,637
1895	28,228

These schools were made up during 1895 in the following manner:

Elementary Schools	26,631
Apprentices' Schools	10
Supplementary Schools for Technical Instruction	55
Blind and Dumb Schools	4
Ordinary Normal Schools	47
Higher Normal Schools	2
Ordinary Middle Schools	96
Higher Female Schools	15
Higher Middle Schools	1
Higher Schools	6
Imperial University	1
Special Schools	47
Technical Schools	50
Miscellaneous Schools	1263
Total,	28,228

At that date 61.24 per cent. of the Japanese who were of a school-going age were receiving, at all events, an elementary education based on modern principles. For the purpose of showing in a plain

PRESENT DAY EDUCATION

manner the extent to which education has permeated in the various provinces I give a special map.* But though this map is clear and explicit, and although in drawing it up I have followed the best authenticated records, I find it exceedingly difficult to derive a satisfactory moral from it.

I cannot say that it illustrates anything in particular, unless it be that it goes to prove that the unexpected always happens with regard to Japanese matters.

Before I went into the question, I was sure that I could have painted those provinces which contain the various treaty-ports black, and have triumphantly called attention to the presumptive fact that the presence of the foreigner had brought with it the inevitable enlightening result, and that these places were the centres from which the educational rays emanated. But although the modern education of the Japanese is primarily due to the presence of foreigners, their presence in given centres affords no guide in localizing elementary tuition at the present day. The figures show us that Yokohama and Kobe are only in second-rate educational districts, whereas Nagasaki is in one of the worst educated provinces—a third-rate educational district —of the island of Kyushu; and this in spite of the fact that Nagasaki is at once the most serious and most successful of missionary headquarters in Japan, that of the French Jesuits.

* This map faces page 70.

Giving up localities occupied by the foreigner as a bad job from the point of view of coloring my map, I took it for granted that Tokio, the present capital, the seat of Japanese enlightenment, the city that holds their splendid university, and a whole quarter full of Protestant missionaries; Kioto, the birthplace of modern education; and Osaka, the great industrial centre, would all come inside the best educated districts in the country.

Alas, Kioto and Osaka are in only second-rate educational districts, and Tokio is worse still — third-rate.

Then I turned to the geographical and geological features of the country for an explanation, but it was not forthcoming. It is possible, I thought, that where the country is mountainous, education will be more difficult than elsewhere, and we shall consequently find the percentages of educated population reduced in those places—but not at all. For there is Fuji, the highest mountain in the country, plumped right down in the centre of a first-class educational district; and there is the island of Hokkaido, the sole remaining refuge of the "hairy Aino," which is given up to snow and ice for some months in the year, is essentially the least civilized of the big islands of Japan, and is full of mountains, but is better educated than the neighboring province of Rikuoku, on the main island.

Then my thoughts reverted to the province of Kii, where it had been my lot to travel for some time, with a view of advising certain owners of forests as to whether it would be possible to overcome geographical difficulties sufficiently to enable them to get their timber to the sea; where my Japanese friend from Nagoya had about as much difficulty in making himself understood by the natives as I had; and where even the Japanese food was so bad that he had a difficulty in eating it; and I made up my mind that, at all events as far as education was concerned, that district could be left white, or nearly so, on the map. Again I was mistaken, for the Government returns show most of this portion of the country to be a first-class educational centre.

In the face of all these conflicting facts, which go to shake one's ordinary theories—for even that proverbial civilizer, the railway, seems to have had no direct influence on the proportionate scale of Japanese elementary education—it is difficult to find a satisfactory reason for the peculiar conditions.

I can only come to the conclusion that, as far as the masses are concerned, education makes more effectual progress in some of the quiet and outlying districts which are practically undisturbed by the foreigner, or by modern methods; where the old native industries flourish steadily and uninterruptedly; where the Japan of to-day is still to a certain extent the Japan of the past; and where the only modernizing influence which is now making itself felt is occasioned by the Government regulations, which insist on a good elementary education of a nature hitherto unknown.

The problem which presents itself, if the above

assumption be correct, is an exceedingly interesting one; for it would seem to imply that side by side with the progressive, ambitious Japan which we know (a Japan which is led still by a comparatively small body of highly educated men, who have a thorough knowledge of the outer world), there is another and equally useful community springing into existence, which in ten or twenty years from now will make itself felt in Japanese politics. I refer to the communities shaded black and double cross-barred on my map, which are made up as a rule, not of men taught by the foreigner, but of those who are being educated quietly and systematically, in the Government and other schools, by their fellow-countrymen, who in years gone by have imbibed their instruction from the foreigner.

The masses who go to make up such communities will in a few years be able, not only to look on matters from a broader point of view than can the common people of to-day, but will understand their political value under existing laws. They should, in fact, eventually form that backbone to the policy of Japan, the voting power, which will solve the future destinies of their country in its permanent modern policy—a power for good or evil, as the case may be, but which is lacking to-day.

Captain Brinkley, who is perhaps our greatest authority on Japanese modern policy, and certainly the greatest writer on the subject, has maintained that the politics of Japan are those of the individual and not of the party. It is to the millions of boys

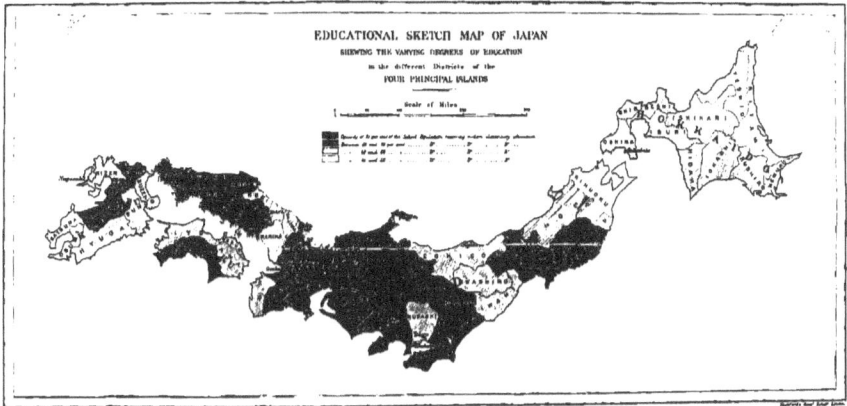

THE ENGINEERING COLLEGE OF THE IMPERIAL UNIVERSITY OF TOKIO
Photographed by Professor C. D. WEST

THE LAW COLLEGE AND LIBRARY OF THE IMPERIAL UNIVERSITY OF TOKIO
Photographed by Professor C. D. WEST

PRESENT DAY EDUCATION

who to-day are partially educated that one must look in the future, when their education has been completed, to furnish the material following of the various political leaders.

Of course the educational map above referred to is only serviceable as showing the general trend of elementary and not of the higher education, and it would seem to show that the big towns, where modern culture is struggling to the front and high-class education is studied, and in the large and go-ahead industrial centres, the masses are not as well looked after as elsewhere.

No doubt this is very largely due to the fact that in such places there is a very large demand for juvenile labor, and consequently the school attendance among the poorer classes is less regular.

Roughly speaking, and in very round numbers, we may estimate that there are in Japan at the present day 30,000 schools of all sorts, 100,000 teachers, 500,000 graduates, 5,000,000 pupils of both sexes; and that the annual outlay, in one way and another, to maintain them has reached about £1,500,000 sterling.

We may also say that at least two-thirds of that portion of the total population who are of school age are receiving tuition of a sort which in quality will compare favorably, as far as their requirements are concerned, with that meted out to the people of any country in the world.

The official description of the Japanese elementary tuition is as follows:

"Elementary schools are designed to give children the rudiments of moral education and of education specially adapted to make of them good members of the community, together with such general knowledge and skill as are necessary for practical life—due attention being paid to their bodily development. The elementary schools are divided into ordinary elementary schools and higher elementary schools. Those established and maintained at the expense of cities, towns, or villages, or of town and village school unions, or of districts within them, are called city, town, or village elementary schools, and those established and maintained at the expense of one or more private individuals are called private elementary schools. An ordinary elementary school course and a higher elementary school course may be established conjointly in one and the same school. In a higher elementary school, one or more special courses in agriculture, commerce, or industry may be established, and a supplementary course may also be established in ordinary or higher elementary schools. The ordinary elementary school course extends over three or four years, and the higher elementary school course over two, three, or four years. The supplementary course extends over not more than three years, while in regard to the special course the length of study is not yet fixed. Elementary schools are also to be established in connection with normal schools."

Turning to the question of the higher education, we find that the list of schools and colleges, in 1896, ran as follows:

University 1
Higher Schools 6
Higher Female Schools 14
Normal Schools 63
Miscellaneous Schools 1352

Since then a second university has been established in Kioto on the lines of the Tokio University. The above institutions, for educating professional men and ladies of corresponding social rank, had between them nearly 90,000 students, 4940 native and 250 foreign professors. Since that date the

PRESENT DAY EDUCATION

number both of schools and of students has greatly increased.

Although the higher branches of modern technical training had been experimented with in Japan at a somewhat earlier period, it was not until 1873, when Mr. Henry Dyer was engaged by the Japanese Government, that a solid system of technical education was inaugurated.

Viscount Yozo Yamao was the Minister of Education at the time, and facilitated as far as possible Mr. Dyer's onerous task of forming the *Kobu Daigaku*, from which sprang the present Imperial University. The work accomplished by Mr. Dyer and his able staff of foreign professors will ever remain less noticed by the world in general than it ought to be, for the reason that it was all carried out so quietly; and, although within twenty miles of a treaty-port, and in the capital of the country, it was out of the regular track of the tourist and the treaty-port resident. The professors, too, who did the work were leading a more or less retired life, as far as the rest of the European world in Japan was concerned.

It is not for me to talk of the respective merits of these men, or to endeavor to point out the amount of influence which their individual labors have had on the modern Japanese character. Among those who have left the country we have such well-known names in the professional world as Airy, Griffis, Anderson, Aston, Dyer, and Milne; while those still remaining, not all now professors, but still living in Japan, have among them Captain Brinkley, Drs. Divers and Baelz, and Professors West, Burton, and Conder.

Mr. Dyer was head professor of the *Kobu Daigaku* until 1882, when he left Japan, and Dr. Divers took his place until 1886, when a Japanese, Mr. Hiromoto Watanabe, was appointed first president of the amalgamated technical schools, which had by this time developed into what is now known as the Imperial Tokio University.

The site of the University is a beautiful one, on high ground, and in a remote part of Tokio known as the Hongo quarter. It spreads over many acres of ground, and its buildings are as a rule large, practical, and in good taste.

At the present day there are about 2000 students of all sorts, and to give an idea as to the scope of their studies, I quote the official description issued by the Department of Education:

"The Imperial University has for its object the teaching of such arts and sciences as are required for the purpose of the State, and for the prosecution of original investigations in such arts and sciences. It consists of the University Hall and the Colleges of Law, Medicine, Engineering, Literature, Science, and Agriculture. The College of Law includes the two courses of Law and Politics. The College of Medicine includes the two courses of Medicine and Pharmacy. In connection with this College there is established a course of lectures on State Medicine. The College of Engineering includes the nine courses of Civil Engineering, Mechanical Engineering, Naval Architecture, Technology of Arms, Electrical Engineering, Architecture, Applied Chemistry, Technology of Explosives, and Mining and Metallurgy. The College of Literature includes the nine courses of Philosophy, Japanese Literature, Chinese Literature, Japanese History, History, Philology, English Literature, German Literature, and French Literature. The College of Science includes the seven

THE SCIENCE COLLEGE OF THE IMPERIAL UNIVERSITY OF TOKIO
Photographed by Professor C. D. West

IN THE QUADRANGLE OF THE ENGINEERING COLLEGE OF THE IMPERIAL UNIVERSITY OF TOKIO
Photographed by Professor C. D. West

PRESENT DAY EDUCATION

courses of Mathematics, Astronomy, Physics, Chemistry, Zoology, Botany, and Geology. The College of Agriculture includes the four courses of Agriculture, Agricultural Chemistry, Forestry, and Veterinary Science. For the training of farmers, junior courses of agriculture, forestry, and veterinary science were also established in connection with this College. For the purpose of facilitating the practical investigations of students and pupils, there are two hospitals, the first and second, established in connection with the College of Medicine. The Tokio Astronomical Observatory, the Seismological Observatory, the Marine Laboratory, and the Botanical Gardens are connected with the College of Science, and the Experimental Farms, the Veterinary Hospital, the Laboratories for Forest Technology, and Horseshoeing, together with buildings intended for sericulture, are provided in the College of Agriculture, also for the same purpose. There are also several other laboratories connected with the Colleges of Medicine, Engineering, Science, and Agriculture. There is also the University Library open to the instructors and students in general. As regards the length of the courses of study, it should be here mentioned that the course of Medicine extends over four years, while in the College of Law no definite term of study is fixed, but three examination periods are specially prescribed for each course. But in all other Colleges, including the course of Pharmacy, the course of study is made to extend over three years for each subject of study. The period for scientific investigations to be carried on by students in the University Hall is fixed at five years, of which the first two years must be devoted to study in the Colleges to which they respectively belong, as postgraduates."

The educational gulf which stretches between the University and the Elementary Schools is bridged by a number of educational establishments graded downward as follows: Higher Schools and Higher Middle Schools, which are preparatory schools for the University; Ordinary Middle Schools; Normal Schools, for the training of teachers; Supplementary Technical Schools; Apprentices' Schools; and Deaf and Dumb Schools. There are also many Kindergartens, and a variety of special schools.

Of female education in Japan it is not the proper

time just now to write, for we may expect very great developments of this in the immediate future. Consequently any details one might give at the present time would be out of date very shortly.

As matters now stand lady students are not attached to the University, nor do they follow a corresponding course of study in any other institution. There are, however, several " Higher and Middle Female Schools," and one school for the daughters of noblemen. A great agitation is on foot with a view of extending the facilities for a higher education of ladies; and practical effect is being given to the growing conviction that as long as Japan only educates her men on modern lines, her progress will only be of a one-sided nature.

There still exists, however, a pious horror in the minds of a large section of the Japanese of the style and methods of the foreign woman, who is looked on as ungainly, unladylike, and immodest; and whose independent and imperious manners are as much misconstrued by the Japanese as—well, as the ways of the Japanese women are, as a rule, misconstrued by us.

In the elementary school girls and boys undergo an identical course of instruction, with the result that among the poorer classes, girl for boy, the one has as good an education as the other; whereas, in the measure as one ascends the social scale, one finds the educational disparity widening between the sexes, an anomaly which, if I am not much mistaken, will soon be remedied now that the Japanese are beginning to understand the problems of modern life. Undoubtedly the greatest personality connected with modern middle-class education in Japan is Mr. Fukusawa Yakichi, who founded the Keio-gijiku, the most important private college in Japan. Of him we read in *Things Japanese*:

"Mr. Fukusawa is a power in the land. Writing with admirable clearness, publishing a popular newspaper, not keeping too far ahead of the times, in favor of Christianity yesterday, because its adoption might gain for Japan the good will of Western nations, all eagerness for Buddhism to-day because Buddhist doctrine can be better reconciled with those of evolution and development, pro- and anti-foreign by turns, inquisitive, clever, not over-ballasted with judicial calmness, the eminent private school-master, who might be Minister of Education, but who has consistently refused all office, is the intellectual father of half the men who now direct the affairs of the country."

Upwards of forty years ago Mr. Fukusawa went to America, and on his return set himself to train his fellow-countrymen. This was before the abolition of feudalism, and his efforts met with but scant appreciation in high quarters, even after the Restoration, all through which troublous times he kept his college going.

A Japanese writer throws an interesting side-light on Mr. Fukusawa's character and methods by pointing out that "During the period when people were discussing the opening of the country, he was already teaching Adam Smith's *Wealth of Nations*. In an age when feudalism was not yet wholly abolished, his students were already reading John Stuart Mill's *Representative Government*."

And the same author points out that Mr. Fukusawa and his students had the unique experience of studying the history of the ancient civil wars and upheavals in other countries, and of simultaneously seeing history repeating itself before their eyes in Japan.

For years after the Restoration the better-class Japanese looked down on Mr. Fukusawa's school and on the students who went there. It was bad enough for gentlemen, who should have been soldiers, to become doctors and lawyers and engineers. However, such men, at all events, went to the University, and did the thing properly. But it never entered people's heads at that time that a Japanese man of good family could descend to banking and other commercial business.

However, Mr. Fukusawa, with his wonderful energy and tact, and his American notions as to what a man should do and how he should do it, fought all these prejudices down, until to-day he stands out above all others as the greatest educational pioneer that his country has ever seen.

Among the private educational institutions which have played a formidable part in instructing the middle-class element is the Christian College at Kioto. This was founded by Dr. Neeshima, a Japanese convert to Christianity, in connection with a group of American missionaries.

Though a highly successful educational establishment, it has deviated from its methods, in the nature of its instruction and the primary objects of its founders; for on the death of Dr. Neeshima, the

MR. FUKASAWA YAKICHI
The pioneer of modern middle-class education

KAWAKAMI OTOJIRO
The modernizer of the drama

PRESENT DAY EDUCATION

Japanese and Americans who jointly managed the institution came to loggerheads; and the former, taking advantage of the fact that the college was built outside treaty limits, turned their American colleagues out of the place, and thenceforth ran the institution on their own lines; still, however, retaining a nominal Christian tendency. This has afforded a painful example of Japanese duplicity, from which the hostile critics of that country have very naturally not failed to deduce many forcible arguments against the methods of the people.

Having now briefly outlined the quantity and quality of Japanese education, it is as well to deal with the capacity of the Japanese as absorbers of instruction.

In this matter I would say at once that I know of no people in the world who can touch them for powers of academic application. Whether their aptitude comes up to their powers of application is a matter on which opinions differ very largely, my personal conviction being that it does.

I have often enough visited the Japanese at their studies of all sorts; in the lecture halls of the Imperial University, and in the humble village classroom; at the rehearsals of their complicated historical dramas, and at the classes for trained nurses in the hospitals; and if application to study may be taken to carry with it a proportionate aptitude for learning, then the Japanese may certainly be said to be capable of giving many points to European and American students.

If those people who, in an airy manner, describe the Japanese as being a light and frivolous people, were to devote a month, or even a week, to looking into their methods of education, they would rapidly change their opinion: an opinion formed on what? Is it on the sights they have seen in a treaty-port tea-house, or on something they have read, and which has been written by somebody who went to a treaty-port tea-house? Have such visitors realized that even in the tea-house in question those very child-like "giggling little girls," as they call them, the *meikos* who dance, and the *geishas* who sing and play the samisen, have gone through a training so lengthy and severe as to make the ordinary course undertaken by our embryo artistes at a musical Conservatoire mere child's play?

If any single proof is required of the hunger that possesses the Japanese for acquiring knowledge, it is to be readily found in the fact that, even when the law of the land prescribed that the possession of a foreign book was punishable by death, there were Japanese to be found not only ready to risk death in procuring such books, but who backed up their eagerness in a practical manner by paying enormous sums of money for them to the philanthropic Dutch settlers who were permitted to reside in Nagasaki on sufferance.

A Japanese friend of mine, who is now a well-known man in the international business world, began his studies of the English language by writing out in its entirety Johnson's Dictionary, a copy of which had been lent to him by a friend. This colossal undertaking he carried out successfully, and when I explain that he painted it all out in Indian ink by means of the Japanese pen, a sort of bamboo brush, on what we should call tissue paper, and when it is borne in mind that at the commencement of his task he was merely copying the outlines of our lettering, the form of which conveyed no meaning to him, the terrible nature of the difficulties he had to contend with, and the tedious nature of his work, can be appreciated.

The late Count Mutsu, who died in 1897, and who had led a life of the strangest vicissitudes, is stated to have started his early studies of the English language by taking a berth as cabin-boy on a British schooner trading between Japan and China.

Chamberlain tells us how, among other adventurous youths, those two well-known statesmen, the Marquis Ito and Count Inouye, years ago smuggled themselves on "homeward (presumably outward from Japan) bound" ships, as affording the only means of gaining a practical insight into the affairs of the outer world, and of learning the English language.

These are only a few examples out of very many that the student of the educational methods of the Japanese must come across continually, and which serve to bring home most forcibly to his mind the fact that, whatever faults there may be in the character of the Japanese, want of application to and enthusiasm for study, even when such study is of a most tedious and heart-breaking character, are certainly not among them.

How far this power of concentration is an acquired virtue, and how far a natural instinct, is doubtless a matter of opinion; but I think that the training of countless generations of Japanese to methodically and accurately base their smallest actions on an observance of strictly prescribed etiquette has developed in them as a race a facility for absorbing study the equivalent of which has only been attained by certain individuals among the Western peoples.

Even among that section of the resident foreigners who do not admit that there is any very great amount of good in the Japanese character, many will allow that they possess this great capacity for absorbing knowledge; but the general impression of such people is that, when knowledge has been absorbed satisfactorily, they have not a corresponding capacity for applying it to the practical uses of life.

In justice to the Japanese it must be admitted that we, the Western foreigners, have not as yet had a full opportunity of judging this question. We notice, of course, their mistakes in modern policy and in administration; and it often strikes us that such errors might have been easily avoided had a European been at the head of affairs. If, however, the proof of their practical capacity is to be found in the grand results of their modern policy, we have to admit that, whatever the sum total of their

A GROUP OF ENGINEERING STUDENTS AT THE IMPERIAL UNIVERSITY OF TOKIO

Photographed by Professor C. D. West

PRESENT DAY EDUCATION

blunders may amount to, they have been swamped over and over again by the general progress which has taken place.

Speaking personally, I have been in contact with statesmen, politicians, diplomatists, barristers, lawyers, doctors, journalists, engineers, and architects, who, looked at from the Western point of view, would be considered thoroughly competent in every way.

Possibly and probably there are not enough of them in all for the qualities of the best among them to be utilized to the fullest advantage, and in judging them we must remember that the thoroughly competent lawyer has to create his modern office staff, and educate the members of it to meet his standard; worse still, the modern Japanese manufacturer, instead of being able to draw his operatives from a large class of artisans already born and bred in the atmosphere of their trade, must, after buying his machinery and equipping his factory in the most up-to-date manner, begin the terrible task of personally educating the whole of his labor; and, worst of all, the first-rate modern politician has to educate the whole of his constituents in the theories of modern politics.

With regard to this last question, we have ample proof of the thoroughness of the Japanese character, when we consider that that remarkable statesman, Count Okuma, even took the trouble some years ago to found a school—possessing, I believe, over one thousand pupils at the present day—in which his particular form of political views are drummed into the heads of the boys simultaneously with the general educational subjects.

Under such circumstances the difficulties of those Japanese who are thoroughly educated in their various professions, in dealing with so many who are not, can be appreciated, for they are in reality living ten or fifteen years before their time.

These, in fact, are the halcyon days of the young professional man leaving college, for in nine cases out of ten he steps straight from school into an important situation such as we should not think of intrusting to his British equivalent until he had had ten or twenty years of hard grinding at his practice.

Thus it is that we find the Japanese making so many palpable mistakes in all sorts of ways in their conduct of modern politics, professions, and business —mistakes which afford an easy target for the critic, but which are due to a want of experience and not to a lack of intelligence; mistakes which are inevitable under the circumstances, and the real cause for wonder with regard to which lies in the fact that a great many more are not made.

One cannot leave the question of education without touching on that feature of it on which Englishmen rightly lay so much stress—that of the body as opposed to that of the mind. Though taken up somewhat late in the day in Japan, modern athletics and games are being propagated with energy and success. The boys and girls, even the youngest of those in the elementary schools, are carefully and

PRESENT DAY EDUCATION

systematically drilled, and encouraged to take part in games. Of these the most popular is base-ball, imported from the United States, and in playing it the Japanese children are both keen and capable.

So thorough are the Japanese in the way they tackle everything that, when small boys are playing, an instructor, thoroughly versed in the intricacies of the game, presides over it, fulfilling the functions of captain, umpire, referee, and general factotum, issuing his orders and counting the balls, and very often employing the English language in so doing.

The University students are so strong at base-ball that they usually beat the foreign teams in their matches in the treaty-ports.

Lawn-tennis, bicycling, and rowing are also very popular; and, as a sign that the official seal of imperial approval has been extended to the policy of athletics, it is well to mention that in a regatta in Tokio no less than four of the Japanese princes coxed opposing crews in one of their important races a year or two ago. I think that constitutes an international record as to royal patronage, in a practical form, at a boat-race. In taking to out-door pastimes, the youthful Japanese of to-day are, in their keenness, style, and appreciation of them, much nearer to English and American boys than are French, German, or those of any other race I know.

CHAPTER V

THE NEW SCHOOL OF DRAMA

To the student of character the theatre is perhaps a more reliable indicator of the real aspirations and methods of a people than almost any other institution. The drama, we are told, "holds the mirror up to nature"; and whether a very polished mirror, or a somewhat tarnished and distorted one, it nearly always offers a recognizable reflection. In Japan, where an insight into the real character of the people is hedged round with so many complications and difficulties, the drama is essentially useful as offering the foreigner a means of either confirming or dissipating his impressions on a given subject.

The old Japanese classical drama is so serious a business that one can understand that many foreign writers maintain these plays to be slow and uninteresting to watch for more than a short time, though personally I have never found them so. It is not my wish to hark back to the classical drama, which subject has been thoroughly well treated by a variety of writers, beyond touching on it sufficiently for the purpose of comparing it with the more modern plays which are springing into popularity at the present day.

THE NEW SCHOOL OF DRAMA

The Japanese have from time almost immemorial taken their theatre very seriously; so seriously, in fact, that any departure from the well-established routine and etiquette was not only looked upon with disapproval, but was considered to constitute almost a species of sacrilege. In Japan, where the essence of religious practice consists in the worship of one's ancestors, and the dramatic performances of the old school have been confined to the representations of episodes, real and imaginary, of mediæval and mythical history, it is only natural that the theatre should have retained a certain semi-official connection with the religion of the country. Chamberlain tells us that the theatre in Japan, as, in fact, elsewhere, owes its origin to religion; that "it can be traced back to religious dances of immemorial antiquity, accompanied by rude choric songs."

However, with regard to the classical drama of Japan, the ordinary educated Japanese of to-day, though conversant with the time-honored and fantastic mythology on which these plays are based, has difficulty in fathoming the stilted phraseology of his theatre, which is quite unlike any colloquial Japanese. Consequently, in spite of the general veneration in which the classical theatre is still held, the need of some more popular, if lower class, entertainment was felt, and this eventually introduced itself in the form of plays having to do with contemporary every-day life. Such performances have been well attended, though professedly looked down upon as vulgar by many of the people who patronized them, and though the actors were spoken of with contempt. But these social plays, though they undoubtedly formed the first step towards the modernizing of the Japanese drama, were essentially Japanese in their theory and practice, and no attempt was made to represent foreign life, beyond introducing occasional scenes in China and Corea.

The great exponent of the old school of drama is, of course, Ichikawa Danjuro, who, though very nearly sixty years of age, is still able to go through daily performances of eight hours' duration without apparent fatigue, and to impersonate indiscriminately men or women of any age and character.

To me the personality of Danjuro was intensely interesting; and on the many occasions on which I had opportunities of conversing with him, in his dressing-room, between the acts of all-day-long representations; at his rehearsals to which he invited me; and at his private residence in Tsukji, he was always extremely willing to give his point of view with regard to the old and the new Japan.

Danjuro's manner is dignified and courteous to a degree, which has doubtless become accentuated by his lifelong impersonations of the Daimios and old-time heroes. I have often thought it strange that he, the actor, the man whose life must essentially be artificial, should have been the one Japanese, of the many in all stations of life with whom I have come in contact, who should the most emphatically impress upon me a conviction—which I feel sure is shared by every Japanese who breathes, although appearances

ICHIKAWA DANJURO
The great exponent of the Classical Drama

would not seem to warrant such an assumption—to the effect that while the Westernizing of his country might be a necessary policy, it was nevertheless a necessary evil.

Danjuro may be taken as the embodiment of the classical drama, and very naturally he is the bitter and very powerful opponent of innovations which may tend to popularize any other class of entertainment. But the day for up-to-date drama was bound to come, and the modernizing of Japan eventually brought it about.

The pioneer in this new movement was an actor named Kawakami, and if comparisons can be made where surroundings are so different, Danjuro may be said to represent the Henry Irving of Japan, while Kawakami fulfils the combined functions of the late Augustus Harris and Charles Warner, with a dash of Coquelin *ainé*. Kawakami has visited Europe, though not England, and he professes to take as his European model rather the French school of acting than the English. However, as he expressed it to me, all the world is his prompt-book, and his aim is to go in for the realistic and modern. As was to be expected, he found great difficulty in overcoming time-honored prejudices and opposition; but the war with China, which opened up so many new channels in Japanese enterprise, gave him his opportunity and he took it. He brought out a piece entitled "The China War," and dealt with episodes of the field of battle, portraying the prowess of the Japanese in a thrilling and sensational manner. In this piece some of the most realistic stage fights that have ever been portrayed took place, and through the piece, in true Adelphi style, ran a tale of individual heroism and suffering.

The thing was well done, the time well chosen, and Kawakami played to crowded houses. But, not content with his success, he went over to China in his search after the realistic, and personally visited Port Arthur and other prominent places where the fighting had been going on. Returning to Japan he modified his piece to suit the events, and finally achieved a great and a lasting reputation for his particular line of performance.

Shortly after "The China War" had been withdrawn, he brought out a far more cosmopolitan and ambitious piece, and one which at the present time, when Japan is opening up her intercourse with foreign nations, exactly suits the temper of the people.

It was described as an adaptation of Jules Verne's *Round the World in Eighty Days*, and, with a view of exemplifying the manner in which the Japanese can handle a modern European piece, I give below an outline of the manner in which it is worked out. It will be seen that Jules Verne's story is recognizable all through, though the conditions are distorted to suit requirements.

Of course the hero is a Japanese, and it is over a game at billiards in the Tokio Club that he makes his wager that he will travel round the world in the stated time. The gentlemen who take up the bet are "made up" in a manner which makes it easy

THE NEW SCHOOL OF DRAMA

for the audience to recognize them as well-known contemporary Tokio celebrities.

The hero takes his departure, accompanied by a low comedy servant (Kawakami), and closely followed by a detective, who mistakes him for a man who has robbed a bank and is wanted by the police. In the hurry of the departure the detective has not been able to secure the warrant for the arrest of the travellers.

At San Francisco the Japanese Consul refuses to grant a warrant, on the ground that "no Japanese gentleman can be a robber." (Loud applause.)

We next have a scene depicting an American railway depot, which is very like a Japanese station, but the crowd is American, and the people are rough and rude, and show their contempt for the Japanese travellers. There is an election fight going on, and the detective comes in for some rough handling until he recognizes among the mob an old friend of his, a Japanese *soshi*, or professional bully, who has come to the United States, as the pay for this line of business is much better there than in Japan, and the work more plentiful. With this man the detective comes to terms, and it is agreed that the hero and his servant shall be hustled by the election gang and prevented from taking the train, the object of the detective being to delay the travellers until he gets the warrant from Tokio to arrest them. After a good deal of fighting, however, they all three catch the train, and, presumably, go in it all the way to India, as the next scene opens in that country, England, France, and Europe generally, and sea-travelling having been skipped over.

In India we are plunged at once into excitement. The travellers, including the detective, who has by this time made their acquaintance, are found in the middle of a dense jungle, and are hiring an elephant for £1000, which they rightly look upon as an exorbitant price. Then comes a funeral procession. A prince has died, and the friendly Indian who has made the bargain about the elephant, and who talks excellent Japanese, tells them that the widow is to be burned alive, in accordance with the Indian custom tolerated by British rule. It turns out that the widow in question is a young Japanese girl, who had been smuggled out of her native country by Chinamen and sold to the Indian prince. This rouses the indignation of the travellers, and they secrete themselves and watch the procession passing. The widow, with her hair down her back, follows the coffin, and is dragged along by a stalwart Indian, who is armed with a big Turkish scimitar. The scene changes to another part of the jungle, with the funeral pyre in the centre, the widow on the top of it, and a ring of Indians dancing round it and uttering incantations. The fire is lighted, and it is so little a stage fire that the whole of the scenery appears to be enveloped in flames, and the entire theatre is actually filled with smoke, until the audience are almost suffocated. But for a moment, in the midst of the flames, appears a huge monster with a hideous face, clasping the fainting widow round the waist. The Indians are filled with superstitious fear, and well they may be, for the fire would have burned up any human being over and over again, and, believing that they had seen the devil, some die on the spot and others run away. After all, the fearful apparition turns out to be the low comedy servant, who has had the happy idea of placing in his master's luggage one of those hideous Japanese masks with which every curio collector is familiar.

In Hong Kong we are introduced to an opium den, with very realistic Chinamen in various stages of intoxication. Here the detective successfully drugs the servant, who loses his master for the time being. Later on we find the servant, who, in the absence of his master, has no money, earning his living in Shanghai as a professional juggler under a Chinese showman. Eventually the three travellers come together again, and they, with the rescued heroine, who by this time is on the best of terms with the hero, arrive in Yokohama. But they have not yet been round the world, as they have to get to Tokio. However, they find that they have just time to catch the last train which will allow them to accomplish their object in the specified time. But their hopes are dashed to the ground, for at this point they are arrested through the machinations of the detective. The despair of the hero is great, and the indignation of the servant extremely comic, as they are led off to prison, when within eighteen miles of their destination, by the Japanese officials, who are "always unbending in their duty." (More applause, though mixed with many tears, by the audience.) Eventually, however, the error is found out, the real robber caught, and the mistake of one day in their calculations is established, so the hero arrives at the gates of the Tokio Club just at the appointed moment, to the discomfiture of the gentlemen who are waiting for him, and who have lost their money, and in spite of the frantic efforts of a mob of roughs who, having also put their money on the wrong side, do all they can by physical force to prevent his arrival.

There is a second lady waiting for the hero in Tokio, who appears to be very much attached to him, but whether she is his wife or not I do not know. At all events she and the new-comer, the widow of the Indian prince, appear pleased to meet each other, and so it is to be presumed that they all live happy ever afterwards.

Of course, the piece is full of incongruities from beginning to end; but, bearing in mind the conditions under which it is produced, it is a wonderful piece of work. The scenery, as is nearly always the case in Japanese theatres, is artistic, and the effects are good. And when it is taken into consideration that the performance is carried on in semi-daylight, and that lime-lights are not used, the difficulty of doing justice to scenery can be appreciated. As an instance of the enterprise of Kawakami in Europeanizing his performance, I would point out that he has trained an orchestra to accompany the various in-

DANJURO AS THE CHIEF OF THE FORTY-SEVEN RONINS
Photographed by GENROKU-KWAN

cidents with European music. I cannot say that it is a very harmonious one, but it is certainly no worse than some circus bands in England. And, when one bears in mind that the musicians are playing mechanically airs which they neither understand nor appreciate, it will be seen that Kawakami, in setting himself the task of modernizing the tastes of the Japanese on theatrical matters, is not shirking any part of his undertaking. The heroine was rescued to the strains of what I believe to have been intended for " The Roast Beef of Old England," while her agony scene, before the fire was lighted, was accompanied by slow music in the shape of " The Last Rose of Summer" turned out on a hand-organ. The performance terminated with " God Save the Queen," possibly because I had been down to see Kawakami in his dressing-room between the acts.

The classical performances do not allow the foreigner to gauge in any detailed manner the qualities of the Japanese actors, though, in a general way, their professional skill has long been admitted. Now, however, that Kawakami is working on European lines, foreigners have a better opportunity of forming comparisons between the acting here and elsewhere. The striking feature to be noted is that all the minor parts are worked out so well, and filled concientiously and naturally. There is no straining after effect, and there is a total absence of what one may term the "pantomime crowd" awkwardness among the supers. The policemen, the errand-boys, and the Indians all looked like natural policemen, errand-boys, and Indians. Even the hard-featured and angular American mob was a fairly good imitation of the real thing, and as they all spoke and shouted and swore on the stage in English and French, the effect must have been even more realistic to the Japanese audience than it was to a foreigner who knew the languages they were trying to speak. Kawakami has not yet succeeded in overcoming the prejudice which exists in Japan with regard to women and men acting together, and all his female parts are taken by young men. He thinks, however, that this change will come with time, and there is no doubt that it would greatly improve the performance if such were the case. Various writers on Japan put this practice of keeping women and men apart at the theatre down to a question of morality, but it is difficult to see how this could have any effect on morals. Any one who has been behind the scenes at a Japanese theatre must have seen many women there. It is quite the usual thing for wives of the actors, as also for their sisters and their cousins and their aunts and female servants to act as dressers and helpers, and it cannot be supposed that the actual presence on the stage of actresses with the actors could make any difference whatever to their moral relations. There are many theatres where women act by themselves, and from the point of view of the public they are in no way inferior to the men as dramatic exponents, but up to the present their pieces are confined to the classical *répertoire* of the country. Kawakami tells me that none of these actresses would do for his class

ACTRESS IN OLD STYLE PLAY
Photographed by GENROKU-KWAN

THE NEW SCHOOL OF DRAMA

of piece, and that it will take some time to educate women specially to take his parts. Danjuro, whom I also questioned on the subject, maintained that there was only one actress in Japan whose rendering of the classical pieces was at all on a par with that of the men who take the women's parts in his theatre. This lady's name is Fukuti, and she is admittedly the best Japanese actress, even for young parts, although she is fifty-three years of age.

The law at one time prohibited men and women appearing together on the stage, and by the time it was rescinded the habit of doing without each other had become so ingrained that it was not found advisable to alter the existing methods. The only concession that Danjuro has ever made in this respect is when he took part in a short play with the French actress, Madame Theo, who was on a visit to Japan. The piece was specially written for the occasion, she acting in French and he in Japanese, and the prompter being an ex-member of the Japanese legation in Paris. Danjuro told me that this was the only occasion on which acting had been an effort to him. There is no doubt that the modernizing of the drama will bring about before long the mixing of the sexes on the stage, for, with the improvements in stage-lighting which Kawakami will find necessary to give effect to his modern scenery, the men who act as women will no longer look as natural in these parts as they do at present. That the theatre on modern lines should have found a footing in Japan is a cause for congratulation, and affords one more sign of the rapid progress which the country is making. That it should oust the classical drama is out of the question, but that it will take an increasingly prominent position may be foretold with equal certainty.

The fact of the matter is that until recently, so long as Japan was shut up within itself, the theatre had to rely on essentially Japanese subjects, historical and otherwise, for its plays. Now, however, that the knowledge of the people is increasing, and they are becoming more cosmopolitan in their views and habits, they require a wider range in their theatrical *répertoire*, which will accord to a greater extent with their aims and ambitions of the present day.

CHAPTER VI

THE POSITION AND PROSPECTS OF CHRISTIANITY

WHEN writing on the subject of the progress of civilization in a country, one cannot very well avoid touching on the subject of Christianity. Many persons hold the view that civilization is the direct outcome of Christianity; a still greater number consider that the one forms an essential feature of the other; and, in any case, it would be a difficult matter to point to a single country of first-class standing, a great Power, which is not, in name at all events, Christian.

If Japan, therefore, is destined to become a great Power, she has to make up her mind either to fall in with the religious views of the rest of the modern world, or to prove her capacity to run satisfactorily on her own religious lines, as the one exception to the rule.

The present state of Christianity in Japan is at once a painful and an unsatisfactory subject to write about. One of the leading Japanese journals recently stated that "when Christianity first came to Japan it was warmly welcomed; in after-years it was bitterly opposed; and, at the present day, it is treated with indifference." And there is no doubt that this short sentence accurately sums up the state of affairs.

When the Dutch, centuries ago, began to preach Christianity in Japan, the people of the country, struck with the profound knowledge and general superiority of their teachers, readily came to the conclusion that the religion of men who could do and tell them such wonderful things must be a better one than their own. At the time, therefore, of the early missionaries there were undoubtedly many thousands of real Christians among the Japanese. Then, with the advent of the Spaniards and French, Papistry and Protestantism were pitted against each other, in the same manner as has for centuries been the case in many countries nearer home, and with the same deplorable results.

The Protestants were able to convince the Japanese that the Catholics were not Christians, and were merely, under the guise of Christianity, plotting against the State. Some were therefore massacred, and the rest driven out of the country.

But the Japanese soon became aware that both Protestants and Catholics were Christians, and they quickly came to the conclusion that, if one branch of that religion could hatch treasonable designs, the other might possibly do the same. The bitter hostility between the two sections of one religion shook the faith of the Japanese in Christianity; and, in that abrupt manner which to the present day characterizes many of her political actions, Japan determined to have no more Christianity, and no more foreigners. When, after the lapse of years, the foreigner was once more admitted to certain treaty-ports, and, under

PROSPECTS OF CHRISTIANITY

stringent restrictions, to other portions of Japan, the inevitable missionary followed in the wake of the business man, and did much excellent work.

At first his task seemed easy. He erected schools, which readily filled with pupils, who were eager to learn everything that the foreigner was willing to teach them. So it looked, on the face of it, as if Christianity were making progress; for this rush for knowledge, and especially for a knowledge of the English language, was mistaken for a rush for Christianity.

Now, the average Japanese has a highly developed desire to avoid hurting people's feelings; and, as an effect of this, when he went to a mission school to learn English without paying for it, he raised no objection to being called a Christian for the time being. He fell in with this practice, from very much the same motive as that which prompts even a freethinker to take off his hat when he enters a sacred edifice. It was the right thing to do, and he did it. But when the pupil left school he left his Christianity, with his school-books, behind him, as a matter of course.

Again, a Japanese is essentially a man who can adapt himself to circumstances, as any one who has seen him out of his country must admit. And it is in the carrying out of this strongly developed instinct that, when a young Japanese goes to Europe, he, by a species of evolution, becomes a "Christian" from the moment he leaves his country until he returns home. The Japanese professor, or other experienced adviser, will say to the young man starting on his travels: "You had better buy a Bible, and go to church when you are away; it may make things easier for you, and cannot do any harm."

The equivalent of the above advice would be found in an Englishman who had travelled saying to one who was about to do so: "When you go to Japan you had better take out a passport. You may or may not have occasion to use it, but it is just as well to have one by you."

Opinions differ widely as to how far the principle of adapting one's self to circumstances is a virtue, and how far a vice; but in England, at all events, to be too accommodating in this way in religious matters is looked upon as being somewhat contemptible. No doubt a Japanese, when travelling, sometimes finds that the policy of pretending to be a Christian may have the effect of rounding off some of the rough corners which he is bound to come across in his contact with some foreigners in the course of his travels; but it is equally certain that he would often be regarded with greater respect by a great many people if, when questioned, he were to admit his real religious views.

The assumed "Christianity" of the travelling Japanese, however, cannot be attributed altogether to hypocrisy, for the modern Japanese man, at all events, has not, as a rule, very strong religious tendencies of any sort. Many of the educated classes have as much knowledge of Christianity as they have of Buddhism, the rudiments of the Christian faith being of a much more simple nature than those of the other; and the rush for modern education having elbowed out many of the opportunities offered in the old days for profound religious study.

Shintoism, which many foreign authorities maintain to be no religion at all, amply suffices for the requirements of the ordinary Japanese of to-day. A faith, which consists in the worshipping of one's ancestors mainly, it is to be presumed on account of their having brought into the world so perfect a specimen of humanity as one's self, is essentially a self-satisfying belief, and one which, if it tends to self-assertion, essentially helps to hold families and the nation together. But there is a want of conviction among the Japanese about religion in any form.

As pointed out above, it is neither ignorance of the subject, nor hostility to it, which has caused the Japanese to eschew Christianity, for the younger generation, at all events, have a more complete knowledge of its doctrines than have many of the half-educated missionaries who go out to teach them. But the heads of the modern Japanese are full of the doctrines of John Stuart Mill, Auguste Comte, and others, whose writings they have studied side by side with the Bible, and it is easy to understand that the materialist philosophy of such authors must appeal strongly to the Japanese, who, in searching after foreign knowledge, are striving to adopt our practical or material qualities rather than our spiritual virtues. Thus it is that the soil is an uncongenial one for a new religion, whatever that religion may be; and again, the Japanese, since their war with China, are so satisfied with themselves, and are so busy in dealing with practical matters, that the moment is not opportune for spiritual innovations.

To attempt to give an accurate notion as to the number of *bona fide* Japanese Christians at the present day would be absolutely impossible. But one may safely say that there is not one in every 100,000 of the population. Missionary statistics, however, do not point to this state of affairs, for the returns still show what purport to be conversions to Christianity. But, unless the good faith of the missionaries is called into question, one must assume that they have been misled into considering that if a Japanese in talking to them did not combat the principles of Christianity he must necessarily be a Christian. Now, when a Japanese is in contact with a foreigner whom he believes to have strong religious feelings, the last thing he would think of doing, as a rule, would be to offer any opposition to such convictions, and the people of the lower classes, until recently, at all events, had no objection whatever to being entered in the missionary returns as "Christians." To such people the form of baptism, as a rule, meant nothing whatever beyond the fact that they were going through an unnecessary ceremony to satisfy the fad of a foreigner, who had perhaps been kind or who might some day be of service to them. The fact of having gone through the form of baptism would not change in any way

PROSPECTS OF CHRISTIANITY

their original faith, if they had any, in their own religion; nor would it strike them that they were expected to exhibit such an effect.

It is to be presumed, therefore, that the returns of "Japanese Christians," which are sent to Europe and America from time to time, comprise every Japanese who raises no objection to being called a Christian to please the missionaries. The number of such "Christians" is no doubt very great, and they may be divided roughly into the following classes:

1. *Professional Christians*, who make their living in one way or another by working for the missionaries.
2. *Interested Christians*, who derive material benefits by falling in with missionary views.
3. *Nominal Christians*, who have been in contact with missionaries, and who for various reasons raise no objection to being so styled.
4. *Temporary Christians*, who are the children and others passing through the missionary schools for purpose of being educated in foreign subjects.
5. *Christians from force of circumstances.* The native wives and servants of such of the Europeans as insist on their dependants observing Christianity; and a portion of the Eurasian population.

The extending education of the lower classes is now, however, beginning to make it clear to them that the form of baptism should carry with it a moral obligation of some sort to change their religious methods; and no doubt it is on this account that there is a growing distaste among even the poorer Japanese to call themselves Christians.

Certain it is that, now that English and other modern subjects can be taught in the Japanese schools, and in foreign schools where Christianity has no place, the missionaries find it increasingly difficult to get pupils. Consequently, in spite of the fact that hundreds of thousands of pounds have been spent on buildings with the idea of utilizing them in the propagation of the Gospel, many of these institutions are now either nearly empty, or in them Christianity has been so wrapped up in other subjects as to convert them into secular schools to all intents and purposes. So that, at the present day, the Japanese is getting tired even of pretending to be a Christian, which is perhaps more satisfactory after all; for, when all pretence has been done away with, there will certainly remain some genuine converts, and it is only then that one will be able really to gauge to what extent Christianity has had any effect.

But, while everything seems to point to the fact that the present day Japanese have no liking for the Christian religion, we cannot shut our eyes to the fact that they have never had an opportunity of seeing the best side of Christianity. Enormous sums of money, it is true, have been squandered by well-meaning people to Christianize the country, but unfortunately this work has been intrusted largely to men who are utterly unqualified, either by education, training, or mode of life, for dealing with the subject.

This may seem a strong statement to make, but, in doing so, I believe I am expressing the feelings even of the accredited representatives of the Church of England in Japan. The conviction that the interests of Christianity are being misused by the missionaries is so strong, that many of the leading Protestant foreigners maintain that the Roman Catholics are the only body of workers who are effecting any real progress in the conversion of the Japanese. The reason for this is very plain. All the missionaries sent out by the Roman Church are thoroughly educated men; they also form a band between whose members there is no sign of dissension. They work in their own way, conscientiously, systematically, and without ostentation; living the lives of the people, on extremely inadequate pay; and the example afforded by the lives of the priests and the sisters is accomplishing results in those parts of Japan, usually rather remote ones, and always in extremely poor districts, where they carry on their work. The *bona fide* Japanese Christian of to-day is, in consequence, a Roman Catholic rather than a Protestant.

There are many good, zealous, and educated men representing the Protestant missions in Japan, but the effect of their work is continually discounted by the mass of uneducated men and women, some of whom are more or less attached to organized missions, and some of whom are merely free lances, but whose actions have done, and are doing, infinite harm to the prospects of Christianity, and especially to the Protestant section of it.

To convey a proper idea as to how this evil exists, it is necessary to explain what mission-work in Japan means. To the English reader the word missionary usually implies a career containing a certain amount of hardship, self-denial, and sometimes even a risk of life. It does not follow, however, that a man may not be a thoroughly good and efficient propagator of the Gospel without enduring hardship. Now in Japan at the present day it is extremely difficult to encounter either serious hardship in the way of living, climate, or extreme filth of surroundings; and risk of life is practically absent. Therefore missionaries may be excused for not being able to find thoroughly disagreeable surroundings in Japan, even if they felt inclined to do so. To use the words of a well-known and much-respected clergyman who has lived many years in Japan, " The life of the ordinarily conscientious curate of, say, an industrial town in England, entails vastly more privation than is the case even with a conscientious missionary in Japan."

One of the great faults of the Protestant missionaries here is that they have not mastered the fundamental principle of Christianity, " Brethren, love one another;" and the consequence is that the time which should be devoted to Christianizing Japan is largely taken up by degrading squabbles between the representatives of the various shades of Protestantism about their respective methods, and the details of their faith. These petty quibbles only tend to lower Christianity, as exemplified by its exponents, in the eyes of the Japanese. The local foreign papers here teem with rancorous letters from

PROSPECTS OF CHRISTIANITY

one missionary to another, often couched in doubtful English, displaying an ignorance of Christian matters, and containing unchristian sentiments. The air is thick with childish and vituperative pamphlets, paid for by the supporters of these missions; and whatever the object of such literature may be, it can have but the one result, of lessening the chances of Christianity in a foreign country.

It is difficult of course to determine what constitutes a missionary and what does not, and often it is urged that many of these half-educated and aggressive preachers are not attached to a "recognized mission." Certain it is that almost all shades, and sections of shades, of Protestant opinion are nominally represented here, some by conscientious men, and some by competent men; but in many cases by a very low class of persons who profess to represent some peculiar religious fad, and whose only method in the propagating of it is to vilify their brethren in Christianity—Protestant or Catholic.

What is the natural effect of this sort of thing on the mind of the intelligent and partially enlightened Japanese of to-day? He is approached by a man far beneath him in intellect and in education, who urges him to forsake his pagan gods and become a Christian. "What sort of Christian?" is the natural rejoinder. "One of your sort, or one of the sort advocated by your brother in Christianity, who sent me this pamphlet last week describing you as a worthless charlatan? Which of the hundred and one sects represented out here am I to belong to?

For you are always casting mud at each other, and I do not know which to believe."

Some years ago, when I was in very close touch with that astute veteran Chinese Statesman, Li Hung Chang, his Excellency had occasion one day to interview an American missionary who had been importuning him on the subject of the outrages on missionaries in China. "Why don't he become a Christian right away, and set a good example?" was the first question put by this enthusiastic divine to Li Hung Chang through the interpreter. Instead of replying directly the Viceroy asked a counter-question, as has ever been his way. This was, "Who was Jesus Christ?" "Why, our Saviour, of course," was the reply. "Yes, yes, I know," said his Excellency; "but what I meant to ask you was, what is the meaning of the word Christ?" The missionary hesitated; then, turning to the interpreter, said, triumphantly: "Guess it don't mean much. Tell him his name is Li Hung Chang, and that don't mean anything; and Christ was called Christ, that's all." "His Excellency says you are wrong," said the interpreter. "Li Hung Chang means 'ever glorious plum-tree' (I think that was his rendering), and he was under the impression that Christ signified 'Anointed.'" "Well," said the missionary, "some people may attach that meaning or any other to it. But He was our Saviour." Li Hung Chang and his secretary exchanged a few words, and then the latter, addressing the missionary, said, "His Excellency is of opinion that if, when you get

PROSPECTS OF CHRISTIANITY

to China, you will place oil on your head, and call yourself 'Christ,' the Chinamen will not know that you are not speaking the truth." To my surprise, the missionary was not at all ashamed of the part he had taken in the above conversation, and proclaimed it on the housetops as illustrative, not of his own ignorance—for the humiliation of being beaten on his own ground had not struck him at all—but as an instance of the depravity of mind even of the educated Chinaman.

I have quoted this instance for the purpose of showing the class of men to whom is sometimes intrusted the propagation of the Gospel from the Protestant stand-point in that part of the world. Such men may possibly do some good in dealing with savages, for they may be genuine though ignorant Christians. The missionary in question was destined to work in China, but there are scores of them not one whit more intelligent or better versed in their subject than the above gentleman to be found in Japan, doing their utmost, perhaps unwittingly, to bring into contempt the faith which they are supposed to be propagating.

I am told that there are not very far short of 2000 paid foreign missionaries, male and female, in Japan; and, as their method of life is so different from that with which one usually associates mission work, it is as well to give a few data with regard to these matters. With the exception of the Catholics, their payment is extremely good. They form their own colonies and their own society, they live in good houses and on good food. Many of them, though paid as missionaries, run a successful commerce in connection with their religious work. In the warm weather the Tokio missionaries migrate in a body to the mountains for months at a time, where they have also good houses of their own, and where they speculate in house property to a very considerable extent.

The American missionaries are so strong a body in Japan that they even have a considerable voice in matters as to who shall hold office in the United States Legation in Tokio. The consequence of this is that they can, and do, give their official representatives a lot of unwarrantable trouble, and materially hamper the political machinery of their country.

These are the sort of men who swamp any good that the conscientious missionaries can do in Japan. For it must be remembered that whether a man is a "crank," or a fanatic, an American lodging-house keeper, a German quack doctor, a Dutch land agent, or an English curio dealer, if he incidentally throws in some mission work for which he is paid, he becomes, in the eyes of the Japanese, an exponent of Christianity, and his ludicrous behavior tends to burlesque and counteract the work of the *bona fide* representatives of the Christian faith.

As a matter of fact, rather than making Japanese converts, the actions of these men tend to alienate from Christianity the sympathies of their countrymen there, or, at any rate, to lessen the incentive to

PROSPECTS OF CHRISTIANITY

religious observance on the part of the foreigners, who do not care to be identified with men of that stamp.

Thus Christianity, in the true sense of the word, as far as the Japanese are concerned, is in as bad a state as it possibly could be, without being absolutely extinct; and the most painful part of it all is, that this has been mainly brought about by a large section of the men whose care it should have been to look after it.

And yet, and this is the irony of fate, there is a distinct possibility that Japan may, within a few years, suddenly become a "Christian" country. Such an eventuality would not, however, be the result of conviction, nor of sympathy with Christianity, nor would it be due to the preachings of the present-day missionary, but in spite of them. Should it take place, it would mean that a law had been passed establishing Christianity as the national religion, and the Japanese people would accept the change without troubling themselves. This would have been enacted from a similar motive to that which has prompted Japan to purchase ironclads, to adopt a gold currency, and to educate her people on modern lines. It would be merely the logical following out of her policy of putting herself on a level footing in all respects with the rest of the civilized world.

Business men all over the world are now leaving no stone unturned to see that their interests are properly served in Japan; and it is high time, if we wish to Christianize the country, that the responsible ecclesiastical authorities in England and America should make a strong effort to see how the interests of Christianity are being served here.

Throughout this chapter I have taken it for granted that it is a desirable thing to endeavor to force Christianity on the Japanese. But any one who knows the Far East cannot gainsay the fact that in those parts of Asia where missionaries have apparently succeeded in making " converts " the practical result has usually been that, in renouncing their own faith, these so-called Christians have merely been reduced to having no *bona fide* faith at all, and have become debased and degraded in the process of conversion to a " Christianity " which is only Christian in name.

CHAPTER VII

THE MORAL STANDARD

THERE is a treaty-port proverb to the effect that Japan is a country where the flowers are without perfume, the birds without song, the men without honor, and the women without virtue. I do not know who originated the saying, but of all the sweeping and unjust statements that have been made of Japan and the Japanese I think that this is the worst. The unfortunate part of it all is that the superficial visitor as a rule accepts it as being true without question; and he does this the more easily as the first portion of the proverb contains a certain amount of obvious truth. As a matter of fact, the above saying begins with the weakest of platitudes and ends with the lowest of libels.

The many writers who have set themselves the task of blackening the moral character of the Japanese may have been acting conscientiously; but I have often wondered which of the ostensibly civilized and Christian nations of the world they have had in their mind's eye as a contrast when they were drawing their conclusions as to the low standard of Japanese morals.

Many of the writers in question have maintained

that this alleged immorality is innate and vicious; while others, who have seemed to wish to palliate or excuse a deplorable state of affairs which, in reality, does not exist more in Japan than elsewhere, have urged as an extenuating circumstance that such want of morals is merely due to that lack of the power of discrimination between right and wrong which those same writers have laid down as being one of the most prominent traits in the Japanese character.

The subject of the morality of any country is a delicate and difficult one to handle, and it is to be regretted that so many foreign writers have dealt both recklessly and roughly with the question of Japanese morals.

In endeavoring to probe most Japanese questions the European must begin by making his mind a blank—that is to say, he should eliminate everything in the shape of prejudice. In studying the language, for instance, his own classics will not help him, either in the construction of phrases or in the meaning of words. In making up his mind to live in Japanese houses he must put away from him all his convictions as to what constitutes comfort, and begin afresh. Then, again, in learning to relish Japanese food, the only thing for him to do is to forget what he has been in the habit of eating elsewhere. So it is with the morality of the country; for if we start from the stand-point that, because such and such a thing is not countenanced in certain other countries it must of necessity be

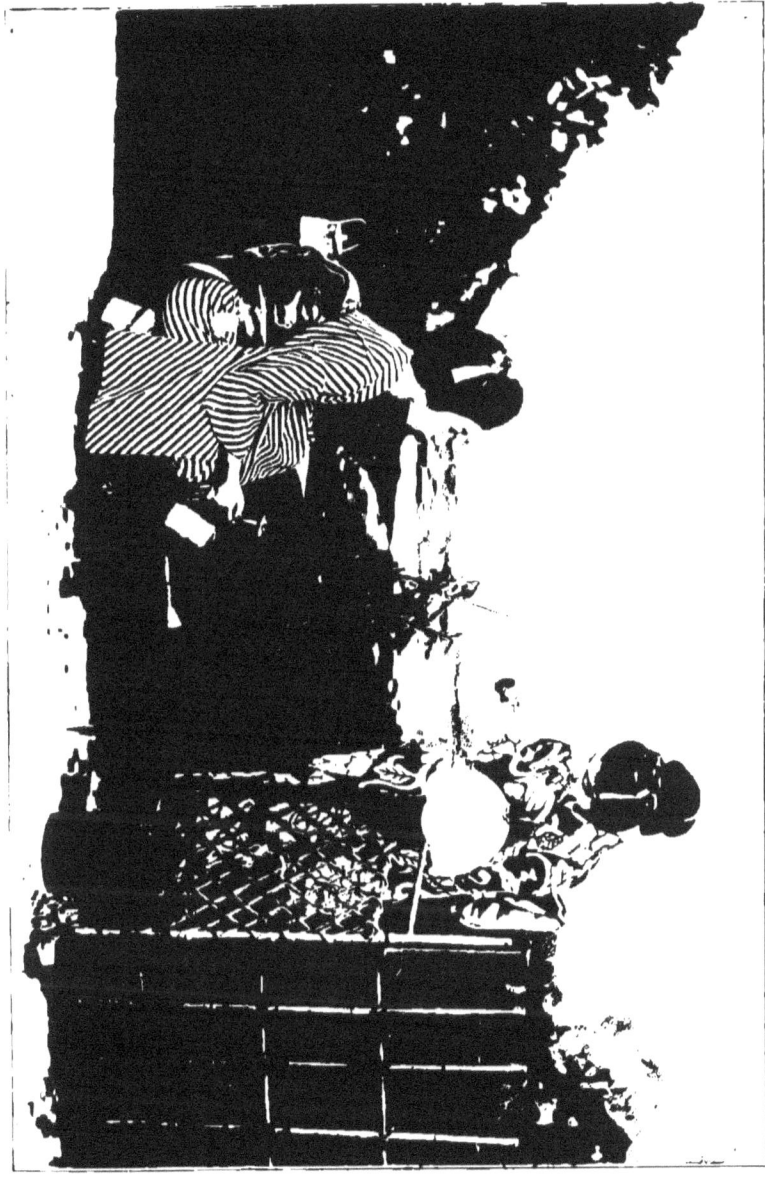

THE MORAL STANDARD

immoral, then there is nothing more to be said, for certainly the Japanese must be immoral through and through.

If we are to assume that our British legal and theoretical codes of morality are perfect, and that we are all in the habit of acting up to the standard afforded by them, then we may claim a right to fall foul of the Japanese with regard to their methods in this respect. But the man of the world cannot for a moment accept either of these assumptions. For if he is capable of reading our contemporary books and newspapers, or of walking in the streets of our larger and, consequently, more essentially civilized towns, he can only form the impression that, however satisfied he may be with himself and his country in most respects, there still remains sufficient room for moral improvement at home to warrant his treating the morality of other and less civilized nations at all events with a gentle hand.

I do not propose in this chapter to compare in detail Japanese morals with those of any individual Western nation, for such a comparison would be practically impossible, owing to the differences in the conditions of life. If, however, one adopts the only fair basis—viz., that of accepting, for purposes of argument, the local laws, religion, and social surroundings of the country—one can only come to the conclusion that the Japanese are by no means less moral than the people of many countries who are wont to exalt their own superiority in this respect. When, therefore, I speak of morality in this chapter,

I am taking it only on its broad lines. I am assuming that morality means the possession of decent instincts, coupled with a modest and respectable demeanor, and, in the case of married people, conjugal fidelity. I am putting out of the question altogether any suggestion that a Church of England marriage ceremony is essential before one can consider conjugal relations of any sort to be of a moral nature. Under such conditions I maintain that while the men of Japan are probably no more moral than those of other countries, the women are certainly no less so, and in many respects afford an example of fidelity and domesticity which might be followed with advantage by their sisters in several highly civilized countries.

And yet it is the Japanese woman who is singled out by the foreign writer as being the type of everything which is light, frivolous, and immoral.

What is the reason of the repeated and cowardly attacks on the character of the women of Japan? I can find but one, and a lame one at that. It must be that their vilifiers have availed themselves fully of the opportunities afforded to any foreigner to gloat over such immorality as goes on in that country, and that they have not troubled to push their studies beyond this point. Such people do not bear in mind that much of the vice that they see in the treaty-ports owes its initiative to the foreigner, that many of the institutions are run to suit his tastes, and are not to be met with in Japan proper. De-

LADY PLAYING THE KOTO

THE MORAL STANDARD

spite this, however, they are all debited to the immorality account of the Japanese nation.

I do not know of a foreign book where an average Japanese lady has been portrayed with any semblance of realism, unless it is Miss Bacon's *Japanese Girls and Women*. The most widely read work of fiction purporting to throw some light on Japanese womanhood, Pierre Loti's *Madame Chrysanthème*, has for heroine a treaty-port unfortunate, who, clothed in a threadbare halo of romance, is palmed off with great skill on the unsuspecting foreigner as a fair sample of the Japanese woman. The heroine of the well-known American song "O Yuchesan" was merely a low-down tea-house girl.

Even the man who has never been in Japan at all does not hesitate to tell us about the Japanese woman, and he tells us she is frivolous and bad. In so saying he is merely plagiarizing others whose knowledge is about on a par with his own and who have held forth on the same subject. Yet it is on standards such as those mentioned above that the foreigner at home forms his estimate of the Japanese woman—he has no other to go on.

In analyzing the morality of Japan one must admit that the laws of the country allow a man to do tolerably well what he pleases in this respect, and that as a rule he fully avails himself of this privilege. Unlicensed immorality is punishable, and severely punished, as far as the woman is concerned, but the man escapes scot-free. But fathers are often extremely severe in the bringing up of their sons, and as a rule paternal authority is far stronger in Japan than in Europe. Thus there are undoubtedly many Japanese men of the better class who lead pure lives in the fullest sense of the word. No doubt such instances are the exception rather than the rule, as is perhaps usually the case elsewhere.

There is a fallacious notion in Britain that the Japanese law recognizes polygamy, or at all events the keeping of concubines; such is not the case. The law takes no more cognizance of the mistress in Japan than the British law does, but Society there accepts her, and, while her children are no less illegitimate than British children would be under similar circumstances, the conditions of life in Japan are such that her position is not a degraded one. As a matter of fact she usually becomes one of the family; and, owing to the peculiar system of adopting children into families which is in vogue and is recognized by the law, their illegitimacy can be, and usually is, overcome.

Family ties and family respectability are such strong features in Japanese life that even the wife will do all in her power to keep both the woman and her children in the house, the former becoming by the process a part of the household, and the maternal authority over the latter being transferred by adoption to the wife. In these circumstances the standing of the *mekake*, as she is called, is a respectable one, and from a Japanese point of view there is no immorality on the part of the woman accepting it.

AN ACTOR DRESSED AS A YOSHIWARA WOMAN
Photographed by GENROKU-KWAN

THE MORAL STANDARD

With the Westernizing of the country, however, the more advanced among the Japanese are beginning to realize that the mekake is no longer a lady to be paraded openly to the world, and there is no doubt that in time to come the prestige of her position will diminish. She will not disappear, but we shall see and hear less of her, and possibly the tendency to legitimize her children will decline. I suppose that we Pharisaical Westerners should find a cause of joy in this, for we shall be able to say that the Japanese are adopting our code of morals. It is true that the effect will be to degrade a class of women who are neither immoral nor vicious in their instincts, and to place their children in an equivocal position. "Never mind," we shall say, "the Japanese are at last becoming civilized and moral."

Many of the priests have mekake as well as wives, and, though this is not considered by everybody to be quite in good taste, the position of the woman is considered an honorable one. Thirty years ago, that is to say, until the abolition of the Shogunate, priests were not allowed to marry, and any immorality on their part in Tokio was punishable by exposure to the insults of the mob in the streets, bound, and in a state of nudity.

To account for the wholesale libelling of the Japanese woman, no doubt the foreigner before arriving has his head full of the immorality of the country, and immediately on landing, for one reason or another best known to himself, he sets about to verify personally the state of affairs. He cannot speak the language, so he takes a guide. The first question his guide asks him is very much the same question that a guide would ask the male tourist in any other country. So he begins his rounds of the treaty-port sights. He visits certain semi-foreign tea-houses, sees a geisha performance or two, and perhaps goes to some less reputable institutions. Then he proceeds to Tokio, and visits the celebrated Yoshiwara.

The Yoshiwara, of which a very great deal has been written, is at once a great and, to the student of character, an intensely interesting institution. It is immoral and cruel; and briefly may be described as the ideal working out to their logical end, and in a practical form, of the theories of those who advocate the State regulation of vice. I have no wish to dwell on the Yoshiwara here. The two best descriptions of this institution are to be found in Chamberlain's *Things Japanese* and Norman's *The Real Japan*. The latter, however, is somewhat sensationally written, and the author makes the mistake of describing it as a "secret institution," whereas, in reality, there is no secrecy whatever about it. It is glaring and obvious to the newest comer, and any journalist who may find it advisable to inform himself as to the inner workings of its organization will have less difficulty in doing so than with almost any other Government institution in Japan. It is, in fact, because the Yoshiwara and the kindred establishments in the treaty-ports can be easily seen that the immorality of the Japanese

TREATY-PORT GIRLS

THE MORAL STANDARD

as a nation is so often grossly exaggerated and misconstrued.

Glaring and obvious, cruel and immoral as these licensed institutions may be, they are, however, all restricted to certain quarters in the various towns, and there is no occasion whatever for any foreigner to visit them or to see anything of them unless he may wish to do so.

However, the foreigner sees them, goes out of his way to see them, and is righteously shocked. Nor does he trouble to ask himself if there are not institutions in his own country, legal or otherwise, which are far more degraded and degrading than the Tokio Yoshiwara.

He has heard over and over again that Japanese ladies and gentlemen are in the habit of selling their children to this and kindred institutions, and that a girl who takes service in these places suffers no degradation in the eyes of her compatriots by so doing. We Europeans consider the Chinese to be very ignorant because they believe that we are in the habit of gouging out and eating the eyes of their children when we get a chance, though these rumors are merely propagated by the official classes in the Celestial Empire in order to foster and maintain the hatred of the masses against the "foreign devil."

But we are equally simple-minded in many of the weird and fallacious beliefs we hold with regard to Japanese customs, and especially with regard to intersexual relations in Japan.

Well, after visiting the Yoshiwara the outraged

foreigner has seen enough to prove to him that Japanese women are immoral, and that is all he wants. No; not quite all. He has heard how easy it is to contract a " Japanese marriage," and he has read in certain imaginative journals some strangely romantic rhapsodies on the Japanese lady. What has he read? Assuredly not that she is a good daughter, a loving mother, a faithful and domesticated wife, and one who within the narrow limits of Japanese customs has been carefully educated. Nor has he read that she is invariably dignified and lady-like, nor that her instincts are wholesome, womanly, and pure. That would have been a plain statement of facts. What he has been told is that she is a species of quaint plaything, a giggling sort of doll, with butterfly proclivities; that she waddles when she walks, always smokes a pipe, and plays the samisen; a being without education, without intelligence, without feelings, and, above all, without morality.

So, with the assistance of his guide, the globe-trotter is introduced to a " lady " who has a " daughter" who is ready to become his " Japanese wife." She is said to be " of the samurai class," and though the foreigner does not know what that means, he has a vague notion that it is in some sort a voucher of respectability, and the " marriage " is effected. The foreigner may be excused for thinking that his companion is a lady, for her manners from beginning to end will be lady-like and modest, whatever her station in life may have been. Now the chances are that she, poor girl, even she, loathing her posi-

PONTA, A TOKIO GEISHA
Photographed by GENROKU-KWAN

tion as she does, will be faithful to her temporary "husband," until such time as he discards her and leaves the country. And then, no doubt, her fate will be to be forced to repeat the process with the next foreign applicant for bogus matrimonial experiment.

It is from this class of union that the globe-trotter draws his conclusions as to the morality of Japanese women. And if one takes into consideration the conditions under which such contracts are made, one can hardly with fairness lay the accusation of immorality wholly on the shoulders of the unfortunate victim of the transaction, who, perhaps, after all, was the only party to the contract who had any just claim to the possession of moral instincts.

Turning from the shallow burlesque of matrimonial relationship above explained to the more serious imitations of the real thing, that is to say, the cases where Europeans have for years lived with Japanese women, infidelity on the part of the woman is admittedly rare; while I understand that the *bona fide* inter-racial marriages offer hardly any instance of female infidelity. If such is the case, what must be the result in purely Japanese *ménages?* In these a husband may, and often does, divorce his wife. But divorce in Japan is not based on infidelity, but on convenience, and Japanese marriages—I mean real marriages—afford an example of female virtue which is far above the standard of that in many more civilized countries.

Conjugal infidelity, so far as the woman is concerned, carries as great a stigma in Japan as it does in England. In fact, if the husband is unfaithful the blame often attaches to the wife, who has not known how to make him happy at home. Nor is the virtue of the married women in Japan insured by shutting them up as in Mohammedan and various other countries. The freedom of intercourse between the sexes is perhaps not quite so unrestrained as in Britain, but it is certainly more so than in countries like Spain, Italy, or South America.

Whatever may be the real state of the morality of the Japanese, we should bear in mind that, while we criticise their doings in a wholesale and brutal manner, and often without any real knowledge of the subject, they, on their part, as a rule, adopt a moderate and inoffensive tone in referring to our failings in this way.

Japanese morality may not be based altogether on the same principles as our own, and no doubt some of us may claim that occasionally the methods in vogue in that country shock our feelings. But in justice to them, before criticising them in a hostile manner, we ought to ask ourselves whether we are not mistaking a frank and clearly defined policy in dealing with what we are wont to describe as " the social evil" for an innate viciousness of character; whether what we habitually lay to the account of the immorality of the Japanese woman would not be more accurately described as the immorality of the foreign man; and finally whether, in holding up the Westerner as a model of morality for the Japanese to copy, we are not clamoring less for an actual decrease in Japanese immorality than for an increase in hypocrisy to cover whatever immorality there may be.

Above all, let us leave the character of the Japanese woman alone unless we have had a better opportunity of judging her than is afforded by a superficial study of the tea-house girl, the third-rate geisha, and their sister of a lower grade still.

CHAPTER VIII

THE COMMERCIAL INTEGRITY OF THE JAPANESE

IT is to be presumed that, as a rule, the business visitor to Japan has made some attempt to study his subject more or less before he leaves his country. He has, no doubt, read some of the import and export returns relating to Japan. He may have also visited some of the merchants in his own country who habitually deal with Japan. Possibly, too, he has had a talk with business men who have been out to that country on similar errands before him.

But the result of all these inquiries will be to leave him in a state of mind which will be worse, as far as complication of impressions is concerned, than the first.

The consular reports will afford him conclusive proof that business, a large and increasing business, is being done with Japan. The London merchant, while confirming that fact, will add that, while it may be just as well for him to go out to see for himself how the trade is done, he would strongly advise him to fight shy of dealing direct with the Japanese, for their business methods are strange.

The business man who has previously visited Japan will endorse and emphasize the opinion of

COMMERCIAL INTEGRITY

the merchant. He will say that the Japanese in business are devoid of integrity.

The man inquiring will, no doubt, ask his informant, " Did the Japanese ever impose upon you when you were out there ?"

" Oh no," will be the reply, " for the simple reason that I did not give them the chance."

" I suppose, then, that your people do not do much business with Japan ?"

" Yes, they do ; and a very large business."

" Then how is the trade worked ? There must be some foreigners who deal with the Japanese direct, and it is to be presumed that the Japanese must pay such people occasionally, as otherwise these transactions would soon cease ?"

" Oh, we receive our payments from the merchants in England."

" Do you refer to the Japanese merchants in London, or to English firms ?"

" Sometimes we are paid by one, and sometimes by the other."

" And do you have much trouble with the Japanese merchants ?"

" Occasionally they are rather fidgety about the wording of contracts and about inspection; but they pay promptly. In fact, as far as carrying on a business transaction is concerned, they certainly give us no more real trouble than do the English merchants, and our monetary transactions with them are quite as safe."

" Then your verdict is that the Japanese traders

in England are honest, and those out there are dishonest?"

"My dear fellow, go and see for yourself. Talk to the Yokohama and Kobe people who deal with them. They will tell you all about the matter."

The somewhat puzzled business man goes to Japan and talks to the treaty-port people. He is told that the Japanese are all dishonest; that they repudiate their contracts; that they will put him to no end of trouble in getting him to give them estimates and particulars; that they will, generally speaking, suck his brains; and that, if he is unfortunate enough to receive an order from them, they will certainly have no intention of paying for the goods when they have been delivered. That, in a few words, is the gist of the treaty-port opinion of Japanese business morality.

If the new-comer should require further confirmation on the subject, he has only to open one or other of the treaty-port papers, and he can in almost any of them read the same line of argument propounded day by day throughout the year. Almost alone among these newspapers to take a different standpoint is the *Japan Mail*, which, though it sometimes criticises Japanese methods, does not adopt the same generally condemnatory tone.

It is necessary to emphasize the treaty-port opinion of Japanese business methods here because it was the treaty-port foreigner, in times gone by at all events, who bore the brunt of direct business contact with the Japanese. If our manufacturers at home have, during all these years, carried on a satisfactory business with the Japanese through his intermediation, then every credit is due to him for sticking to his post under such unsatisfactory circumstances. In fact, it would seem that, by taking the risk of such transactions off the shoulders of our manufacturers, he has been almost heroic in organizing and maintaining the trade between Japan and the outer world.

Every credit, therefore, is due to him for having done this, and his opinions on the subject of Japanese business methods demand a great deal of respect and consideration.

There is no doubt, however, that the treaty-port people in Japan have rather got into a habit of unduly bewailing their lot, partially, no doubt, because they are unaware of, or have forgotten, the fact that in most other countries our traders have, as a rule, to face quite as many and as serious business difficulties, although the nature of such difficulties varies with varying circumstances.

The foreign trader in Japan is often wont to regret the fact that he is not in China, for he maintains that the Chinese are conscientious and ideal traders. It has become proverbial that, as traders, the Chinese are honest, and that the Japanese are not; and no doubt on the face of things it would appear that such was the case. But we must not lose sight of the fact that the conditions of trade between the foreigner and the Japanese are not in the least similar to those in vogue between the foreigner and the

Chinese. It is urged, on the one hand, that a Chinaman's business word is as good as his bond, and that both are good; whereas it is said, on the other, that the bond of a Japanese trader is as worthless as his word in his dealings with a foreigner; for it is alleged that, while he does not hesitate to break a verbal contract, he looks upon any written document as a mere empty formality. Certain it is that such document will be practically worthless in assisting the foreigner to recoup himself legally.

The intricacies of the Chinese character have been very ably dealt with in Colquhoun's recent work, *China in Transformation;* and to those who wish to study that subject I would recommend a perusal of that work.

Suffice it for me to say that, if the Chinese are honest in business, it is the only sphere of honesty in which they excel. It is generally admitted that official and high-class Chinamen are dishonest in their politics and their administration. With them bribery, corruption, extortion, and every other commercial vice are accentuated to an extreme degree, and it is certain that there is a no more accomplished and persistent thief in the world than the lower-class Chinaman.

Then how is it that the Chinese trader who deals with the treaty-port foreigner turns out to be an ideal of all that is honorable in business matters, as we are so often told? The simple answer to this question is, that until now the Chinaman has been absolutely in the foreigner's hands.

COMMERCIAL INTEGRITY

The Chinaman who makes his money in a treaty-port has no greater fear than that of having to take his capital and his business into China proper. He knows perfectly well that, if he makes money and establishes himself outside concession limits, he will promptly be robbed of his wealth by the mandarin and other local officials. Consequently he starts his shop or his factory and invests his capital in the treaty-port, where he will be free to make as much money as he likes without molestation as long as he conforms to the ordinary business routine. His honesty may therefore be said to be an honesty which is bred from force of circumstances; for, if he were to make the treaty-port too hot to hold him, the chances are he would be a ruined man.

Such a state of things does not, however, hold good in Japan, for the Japanese establishes his business in the interior in most cases, and only carries it on in a treaty-port when he finds it handy for his trade to do so. The Japanese trader has no fear of being robbed either by his Government or by the servants of the Government. And the dishonest trader is perfectly aware that he is, practically beyond the reach of the foreign creditor when he is outside treaty-port limits. Consequently an unscrupulous Japanese in the interior has great scope for imposing on the foreigner, if he wishes to do so, provided he can persuade such a man to deliver the goods beyond treaty limits on credit; for, whatever the law may be, in practice it turns out that, by the very fact of the goods in question leaving the treaty-port, the foreigner loses all legal hold on them.

It is true that if a foreigner who has been imposed upon by a Japanese in this manner can get hold of him, he has a right to sue him before a Japanese tribunal, and when this is done he often wins his case. But a dishonest defendant under such circumstances merely has to keep out of the way for a time.

Until recently, too, the Japanese law was of a nature to give the dishonest native dealer who had been sued and had lost his case a further very easy loophole of escape; as, by a simple process, he could transfer in a nominal manner all his property to a friend at short notice. Such a friend had merely to hold the property in question until the foreign claimant had grown tired of claiming in vain, and so the affair would blow over in course of time.

This law has, however, been materially modified and improved lately; and, consequently, if the Japanese tribunal before which the case comes is a competent and just one, the chances of the foreigner in dealing with a doubtful Japanese customer can be said to be materially better than was the case a few years ago.

With regard to the justice to be expected from a Japanese court, I quote below from the *Japan Mail* the results of the law-suits in Yokohama which occurred during the six years ending in 1896, in which foreign plaintiffs sued Japanese defendants before a purely Japanese tribunal. In all there were

COMMERCIAL INTEGRITY

106 law-suits, and they resulted in the following manner:

Given in favor of the foreign plaintiff	36
Given in favor of the Japanese defendant	20
Given partly in favor of plaintiff and partly in favor of defendant	8
Compromised	2
Nonsuited	1
Withdrawn (presumably settled out of Court)	34
Not yet settled	5
Total	106

Out of the twenty cases in which the Japanese defendants won the day, five of the actions were brought by Chinese subjects and two of the cases were practically identical, so that, as far as white, or civilized, plaintiffs are concerned, out of fifty cases in which a definite verdict was given for one side or the other, the foreign plaintiff gained thirty-six and the Japanese defendant fourteen. From this it would not seem that the foreigners have a great deal to fear from Japanese law, and, at all events, they will be better off under it than they are in many other countries where extra-territorial rights have never existed.

But there is a circumstance which must be taken to materially detract from the somewhat rosy picture drawn by this schedule; and that is that, owing to the above-referred-to difficulty of putting one's hand on a defendant after a verdict had gone against him, many foreigners who would otherwise have sued did not bring actions at all, feeling that by so doing they would be merely throwing good money after bad, even if they were to gain their case. Matters, however, are better than this to-day, as Japan already possesses a legal code which in most respects compares favorably for equity with that of almost any other country, and year by year the Government are improving their methods of enforcing their laws effectively.

Political and administrative integrity in Japan is undoubtedly high. It is not, of course, ideal, but, comparing Japan with many countries whose civilization has been brought about by the slow growth of ages, the methods of her politicians and statesmen are less open to reproach than those of half the countries in Europe, to say nothing of those of the Western hemisphere. Again, the lower classes, the smaller tradesmen, servants, and so on, with the exception, perhaps, of those in and near treaty-ports, are, as such people go in other countries, distinctly honest. To account for the alleged dishonesty of the Japanese in their dealings with the local foreigner, we must remember that as a nation they have until quite recently been a fighting, an artistic, and an agricultural rather than a trading people, as we understand the word. In Japan, not so long ago, a trader was a person to be treated with contempt; and, when a certain class is habitually looked down upon in any country, that fact is not at all conducive to a high code of morals in the methods of the men of that particular class.

Again, recognized authorities on Japanese character maintain that one of its strongest traits is an

COMMERCIAL INTEGRITY

instinct and capacity for intrigue. Such being the case, it may be presumed that, now that modern business is conducted by educated Japanese, this spirit of intrigue has been brought to bear, often quite unnecessarily, in their business methods. This may account for some of the alleged want of business integrity in the nation.

Another undoubted reason may be found in the fact that, rightly or wrongly, many of the Japanese in their rapidly acquired Western knowledge have jumped to the conclusion that modern business is based on sharp practice; and it must be admitted that they have every excuse for having fallen into such an error. The Japanese of the present day follow the current literature of Europe and America very closely, and they can see enough in the journals of many civilized countries to convince them that colossal financial and commercial swindles are in many well-known centres quite the order of the day. Then, again, in their dealings with the foreigner it has not always been the latter who has been the honest man in the transaction; and while, as a rule, the Japanese have been as well served as one could expect, they have undoubtedly from time to time individually and collectively been robbed by some of the people from whom they have acquired their impressions of Western business methods.

Of Japanese intrigue in business many forcible instances came within my personal knowledge while I was studying industrial matters out there. One of these, which gives a very good idea of the complicated methods sometimes adopted by them to secure unexpected ends, I give as a representative case. It was part of my duty, when writing on engineering subjects, to inquire into the reason why certain large Government contracts of a kind which had hitherto been habitually placed in England had suddenly been given to another country, which country we will call " X." It is true that time of delivery was in favor of the country X, as the big engineers' strike of 1897 was going on in England at the time; but this consideration, though weighty, was not quite sufficient in itself to account for the sudden and complete change of market. The English firm was represented by a powerful Japanese merchant who could usually get these contracts when he wanted them, and the competing maker in X had a peculiarly sharp representative specially living in Japan for the time being. His firm had given him instructions to do absolutely everything that was necessary to obtain orders, even to underquote when advisable. The great difficulty was to find out what other people were quoting, as the tenders were dealt with in the usual formal manner. By judicious bribery and corruption, however, the smart agent suborned an employé of the Japanese merchant firm to give him the above information, and consequently he was always able to place his quotation slightly below theirs, which resulted in his getting all the orders. But the interesting part of it all was that the Japanese merchants, knowing that they could not get a reasonable quotation for delivery from England just then, did not wish to receive these orders. But not wishing to offend the Government by refusing to quote, and not wanting a competitor to make money on the transaction, they had instructed their employé to be suborned, and to mention to the enterprising agent a price very far below that which they would have quoted, if they had not known that he would go a little lower than the figure they named. So the trade of the country X was extended, and this was duly notified with becoming gravity in the consular reports. British trade had suffered, and the manufacturer of X lost heavily on all these contracts. But the enterprising agent presumably received his commission from the firm in X, and the money he paid with the notion that he was bribing a Japanese employé presumably found its way into the pockets of the competing Japanese merchant firm.

It is difficult to point a moral from the above history. Who was the honest man, and who was the villain of the piece, in this transaction? Did virtue triumph in the last Act or not? If there was any virtue about it, I am inclined to think it did. For the English firm could not have completed the contracts if they had got them at that time; the Japanese merchant and the foreign agent both exercised much ingenuity, and were both rewarded pecuniarily; while the firm in X lost no end of money over these contracts for the sake of the honor and glory of ousting the British from a regular market. Perhaps they too, in the long-run, will get their reward.

Whatever the experience of the local business

foreigner may be, there can be no doubt that the Japanese have, as a nation, a stringent and binding, though possibly from our point of view an inexplicable, code of honor. Our ablest authorities on matters Japanese are agreed upon that fact. The elaborate system of formal suicide (now abolished) in cases where men had violated that code—though looked at from a European point of view as a very barbarous proceeding—is in itself enough to make clear the existence of a strong sense of honor. There is no occasion for me to endeavor to elaborate the details of that code in these pages, as Mitford, Hearne, Chamberlain, and others have made this matter abundantly clear.

Honor, however, is not at the present day absolutely synonymous with business honesty, and in judging how far it may be considered to be so, even in the countries which are accredited with the greatest share of enlightenment, we should not lose sight of the fact that there are many highly "respectable" and nominally virtuous men, who would be extremely disconcerted if they were told that they were dishonorable because, in carrying on their successful business, they considered themselves honest merely on the strength of their having habitually kept just inside the bare letter of the law.

The go-as-you-please arrangements which in the old days existed between the purchaser and the seller in Japan—that is to say, the absence in their negotiations of what we should describe as a hard and fast bargain—do not at all lend themselves to modern business. This was all very well in transactions relating to local produce, and where both parties to the contract were Japanese, and each understood the standing and methods of the other; but it is quite another matter in international commerce.

A Japanese, it is maintained, and sometimes perfectly justly, does not understand the binding nature of a modern business contract, nor has he grasped the fact that there is, or at all events should be, a certain standard of honor in international commercial life, even if such a virtue be prompted by a no higher motive than that which gave birth to our well-worn proverb, "Honesty is the best policy."

I am bound to say that I do not think that the Japanese, in their transactions between each other, are more dishonest than the people of other nations, nor do I think that the shop-keeping class, even in dealing with the foreigner, are nearly as unscrupulous as is usually the case elsewhere. It is, however, the man who carries on the larger negotiations, more particularly with regard to ordering goods from abroad, of whom the greatest complaints are made. And even here I believe that most of the unsatisfactory transactions have been due to a misunderstanding on both sides, rather than to a want of honesty on either side.

We must bear in mind, on the one hand, that the foreign treaty-port trader neither reads nor writes Japanese, and that, with rare exceptions, he does not even speak the language sufficiently well to carry on an intricate negotiation satisfactorily; and, on the other, that the Japanese purchaser has not always been able to know whether he was applying to a specialist in a particular line or not, and that he often did not know what he was purchasing. The result is that both parties have been in the hands of a Japanese business tout, who might or might not be an honest man, and who might or might not be a capable man, if he happened to be honest. These facts, more than any other, have been responsible for the wide-spread impression as to the general want of integrity among Japanese business men. But while such drawbacks to trading on an intelligent basis exist, one cannot be in the least surprised that international business is muddled, and that the local foreign trader, who brought out expensive shipments of goods on what he believed to be a definite order, has sometimes been disheartened.

Nor is it the least surprising, under the circumstances, that, apart from the question of the ardent nationalist instinct, which is so prominent a trait in the Japanese character, the native firms, whose members have during recent years been thoroughly educated abroad in Western languages and business methods, should do all they can to oust the local foreigner, and to conduct the international trade of their own country themselves, even when they cannot always do it satisfactorily. Such firms have not yet reached by any means perfection in such

COMMERCIAL INTEGRITY

dealings, but no one will accuse the better ones among them of repudiating their contracts with the foreigner or of not meeting their pecuniary liabilities. In fact, it is safe to say that at the present day European manufacturers are just as willing to receive their orders for Japan through one or other of the recognized Japanese merchant firms as they are through firms in the hands of their own compatriots. Whether the Japanese user will be as well served under such circumstances as in the past is a different matter, and one on which opinions naturally differ.

The local business foreigner has undoubtedly a very great deal to complain of, and will be increasingly hampered as time goes on in conducting his business in Japan, for he is unfairly handicapped in many ways, as I have endeavored to point out in another chapter.

But his difficulties are not so much due to the business dishonesty of the Japanese traders of the present day, as to the unfair conditions surrounding foreign trade in that country.

To sum matters up: The Japanese code of business morality differs in many respects essentially from our own, and, in default of understanding each other's methods, each party has considered that he has been imposed upon by the other. The new generation of Japanese business men, however, are beginning to grasp the general lines of modern business, and are acting on them with great ability. It is to be feared, however, that sometimes this ability is directed in the wrong channels, and that some of them have taken as their model the methods of the sharp-practicing rather than of the scrupulously honorable trader ; but this is not always the case.

CHAPTER IX

INTERNATIONAL BUSINESS RELATIONS

PEOPLE who wish to make a mathematical study of the figures relating to Japanese imports and exports can obtain them without difficulty from the periodical consular reports on the subject. Such statistics have of late years been very comprehensive and complete, as far as Japan is concerned; and more particularly those issued by the representatives of England, the United States, and Germany.

In this chapter, therefore, I have avoided statistics as far as possible, especially in their tabulated form; for my purpose here is to endeavor to make clear a few of the extremely complicated features in Japanese trading, as carried on with the outside world.

As far as exports are concerned, very little need be said, as there is nothing particularly new, unusual, or complicated in the relations which obtain between the Japanese seller and the foreign purchaser. Japanese rice, silk, matting, tea, curios, bamboo work, and paper, and the hundred and one other products which are familiar all the world over, undergo the same routine as was the case twenty and even thirty years ago. Such trade is to a great extent retained by the local foreigner, who has had, and still has, greater facilities for disposing of the goods in question than have the natives; and at the present day it is as an exporter from Japan rather than as an importer that the local foreign merchant makes his money. Whether such a state of things will continue one cannot say. Personally I anticipate that the rapid growth of the Japanese mercantile marine, and the wonderful extension of the ramifications of the big Japanese merchant firms in all the corners of the earth, will, in the course of time, have the effect of ousting the foreigner to a very marked degree; for there are few foreign firms that have the wealth necessary to compete against the Japanese merchants successfully in the long-run. Or, to put it in other words, those who possess such wealth will find it far easier to get a more profitable employment for their capital in other countries.

It is, however, the import trade of Japan which interests the foreigner out of Japan—that is to say, the home manufacturer, and especially the Englishman; for, while we find it an easy matter to purchase any Japanese goods we may require, the problem which puzzles us is that which concerns the best methods of maintaining and increasing our sales in Japan.

Before dealing with these methods, however, it is as well to try and explain some of the conditions surrounding international commerce.

Speaking generally, during the last twelve years the exports from Japan of *manufactured* articles have increased tenfold, while the imports, which are

INTERNATIONAL BUSINESS RELATIONS

practically all manufactured goods, have about quadrupled themselves during the same period.

Now, the bulk of these manufactured exports have been made by machinery imported; and consequently the large increase of manufactured imports, which, except for war material, are composed mainly of machinery, railway materials, and other productive plant, points to the fact that the capacity for increasing the exports of manufactured goods will be maintained proportionately for some time to come. This may, no doubt, seem alarming to people who deal in articles which compete with those now turned out by the Japanese; but, whether it is satisfactory or not, such a state of affairs forms a complete answer to those who maintain that there is no *raison d'être* for that powerful mercantile marine service which Japan has been organizing so steadily of late years.

In dealing with the methods of importing, I propose to lay stress on one section of it, as by so doing the question is somewhat simplified for both reader and writer. For this purpose I have chosen the engineering trade, which is at once the most important and most difficult. It has, however, the advantage of possessing features covering all the difficulties which beset the commerce in other industries.

From the point of view of the European manufacturing engineer, the most valuable work to be had from Japan is the Government work. For not only is there more of it than all the private contracts put together, but if a certain manufacturer is favored with Government contracts he will, as a matter of course, receive a great many others; for the Government as a purchaser is generally the model on which the private purchaser in Japan bases his policy.

On general lines the private purchasers are logical in so doing, for undoubtedly the Government, with their many engineers and other employés who have been sent to complete their technical education abroad, understand a great deal more about purchasing than does the private individual with his more limited experience.

A few years ago the Japanese Government found it advisable to order most of their material through foreign firms in the treaty-ports, and, as a rule, they were well enough served. But, as time went on, the big Japanese merchant firms and banks not only grew bigger, but began to educate their own people in foreign business much as the Government had been educating their technical staff. Then these merchant firms took over some of the Government technical men and a skilled European or two, and determined to make a bid for the work themselves. The Government, however, got on better with the treaty-port foreigner than with their own countrymen, for he understood the work better than his Japanese competitors; or, at all events, he carried it out more satisfactorily. The Japanese, however, worked very hard and conscientiously to oust him, but were only partially successful.

INTERNATIONAL BUSINESS RELATIONS

Up to that time the Japanese business man, with the exception, perhaps, of those occupied in agriculture, was not only not represented in Parliament, but took no interest in politics. Then came the war with China, and after it the nationalist cry of " Japan for the Japanese." Well, we have heard of " England for the English," and even those of us who admire the notion in the abstract have come to the conclusion that there is nothing in it in practice from the point of view of a progressive country.

In Japan this fact has not, as yet, been fully realized. The Japanese business man, however, one day suddenly discovered that the business men in other countries had enormous political power, and when once he became convinced of this he determined, not unnaturally, to apply this power to his own country. He did not want to bother himself about taking an active part in the administration of politics, but he determined to make use of the political lever, which is strong in every country in measure as the class making use of it is backed up by the possession of wealth, for the purpose of forwarding his interests.

The Japanese merchants considered that their interests would be served if they could effectually boycott or, at all events, seriously hamper their competitors, the local foreign merchants, and they set themselves to use their efforts to further these ends.

Briefly explained, the Japanese merchants were strong enough politically to cause a law to be passed, to the effect that Government contracts for plant and material were to be given only to Japanese subjects. This was ostensibly brought about on patriotic grounds.

It was desirable, too, that Japanese subjects taking such contracts should be financially sound; and the Government provided for this in a very practical manner. The law only allowed such people to quote as had been in business for a certain number of years, and who had habitually paid a certain sum as income-tax. That was right enough in a general way, but the sum stipulated was so great as to put it beyond the possibility of any but an extremely small number of firms to enter the lists at all. Then, as if this measure were not sufficiently harsh, it was further enacted that any one quoting for such work must deposit a sum equal to about five per cent. of the total contract, such contracts often amounting to hundreds of thousands of pounds; and, finally, that, when an order was placed, the contracting party had to increase this deposit to double the amount. The whole of this amount was to be forfeited in event of any slight technical hitch occurring which might contravene the stringent Government regulations as to delivery, and so on. In spite of all these precautions, however, the foreign firms did not altogether lose heart. If they were willing to fall in with the above stringent conditions, they were still able to quote by passing their quotations through a Japanese man of straw, in whose name the deposits were made and the contracts taken. But the worst was to come.

INTERNATIONAL BUSINESS RELATIONS

The Government, while employing inspectors of plant in the countries where such plant was made—and it is to be presumed that such inspectors were competent men—issued an enactment to the effect that all plant was to be reinspected on arrival in Japan, and accepted or declined as the case might be, at their option, and after it had been passed by their own inspectors elsewhere. This of course threw a terrible risk on the shoulders of the merchant contractors, whether native or foreign, as it was not to be expected that the manufacturers in far-off countries would take orders on such terms.

British manufacturers set their faces against this measure from the start; but both German and Belgian firms, in their endeavor to oust British trade, have accepted the risk from time to time; though I understand that they are getting tired of doing so now.

To bring home the serious nature of the liability entailed by accepting the local-inspection clause in Japanese contracts, I quote below a portion of an article which I wrote from Tokio for the *Engineer*, on the " Government Inspection of Machinery," in November, 1897:

"Manufacturers in England of the better class, whose machines are accepted with but a cursory examination in nearly all parts of the world, would be amused at the process to which their best of tools are subjected on arrival here. It is no unusual thing for the machines to be pulled entirely to pieces, and for the whole of the paint to be scraped off the surface of the castings and other covered parts. This portion of the work is carried out by more or less unskilled labor. Then comes a more technical man with a pot of paint and a spiked hammer, and he minutely examines every inch of the surfaces and taps them all over. With a small brush he encircles with a line of paint every imaginable mark that there may be on the surface of the metal. Any little superficial roughness in an unimportant place will be marked, and I have seen often enough slight seams and hammer indentations painted round, on the supposition that they were serious flaws. It does not follow that they will be considered as such at the final inspection, for I had occasion to examine, among other things, some steel flues for marine work, which were obviously good in every way, literally covered with hundreds of painted rings, each one indicating an imaginary flaw. These flues, after a great deal of delay and expense, were finally accepted.

"To give an idea as to the risk that a manufacturer runs in accepting the local-inspection clause with regard to goods for Japan, I cannot do better than refer to the large contract that was given out for cast-iron pipes for the Tokio Waterworks. The contract in question amounted to about 16,000 tons of pipes and bends of all dimensions, from four feet diameter downward. The order was divided among two British firms and one Belgian firm. The Belgian house put in a very low figure, and received an order for 10,000 tons out of the 16,000 tons, including all the special work in the way of bends. Of the 10,000 tons of Belgian pipes only 2700 tons were accepted, and of the English, 4000 tons out of 6000 tons.

"The greatest sufferer by the above transaction is the Belgian manufacturer, who took the risk of inspection in Japan on his own shoulders, and now finds himself saddled with three-fourths of his goods after delivering them half-way round the world. The risk of the British pipes was taken by two firms of merchants in Japan, who supplied the goods in question, one being an English and the other a Japanese house.

"There is no doubt that, with the exception of a small percentage, the rejected pipes, whether or not they filled the specification to the letter, were perfectly good for the purpose. The Belgian pipes were somewhat rough-looking, and not always very close in the grain; but any one having occasion, as I did, to go through the acres and acres of ground covered by these rejected goods could only come to the conclusion that a gross injustice has been done all round.

"Apart from the loss to the contractors, it is estimated that the inspection alone has cost the Government between £5000 and £6000. One is not surprised to learn, under the circumstances, that now that the Government are obliged to ask for further tenders not a single firm, with or without a reputation, will quote.

"It may interest your readers to know how this particular inspection was carried out. When the pipes were put on shore they

INTERNATIONAL BUSINESS RELATIONS

were attacked by an army of coolies, who rolled them about and mercilessly applied the inevitable paint-brush and spiked hammer all over their outside surfaces; and wherever the diameter of the pipes was large enough to permit a thin man to crawl through them, the same process was repeated on the inside. In cases where the pipes were too small for this to be done, their internal surfaces were examined by means of candles on the ends of sticks. As each individual pipe had to be treated in this manner, the process naturally took some time and manual labor. However, when this had been satisfactorily completed, and the pipes had assumed a generally spotted appearance from the lavish application of paint, a gentleman, armed with a microscope and efficiently aided by a staff of candle-bearers, and men with more spiked hammers, probes, and appliances for cleaning the surface of the metal, minutely went over the ground again to satisfy himself as to which of the marked spots indicated a serious defect — *i.e.*, a defect within the literal meaning of the specification. This operation brought into play a second handling of each individual pipe. But this was not the end of all things, for every pipe had to be callipered throughout its entire length, and at not less than four different points. If it was found that in any part the thickness was below the specification requirements the pipe was totally condemned, unless the thin portion happened to be something above half-way down its length, in which case the offending portion might be cut off, and the shortened length only taken over at a reduced price and by weight. . . . Unless a manufacturer is prepared to undertake to accept these conditions, or can get a local merchant to accept them for him, it is not worth while making a contract for pipes at the present day with the Japanese Government."

In justice to the Japanese Government, it must be admitted that these severe conditions as to inspection are enforced, nominally at all events, with equal severity whether the importing agent is a Japanese merchant or a foreigner. But the Japanese merchants, no doubt, to a great extent on account of their nationality, have facilities for getting over these difficulties which the foreigners have not, and they have many methods of recouping themselves on one contract for losses they may have sustained on another. Consequently the Japanese merchants find themselves prepared to take all sorts of risks which a foreign merchant may naturally not care to face.

It is alleged, too, though I am not in a position to say to what extent it is true, that the native merchants used an unjustifiable influence to bring about the rejection of goods imported by foreign firms. Whether such a state of things exists to a marked degree or not, it is clear from the other facts I have given above that the path of the local foreign merchant in Japan is not altogether a smooth one as far as the import trade is concerned, and it is clear that if in the face of all these difficulties he manages to carry on a trade which is mutually beneficial to himself and his compatriots at home, the manufacturers, he deserves a very great deal of credit. He deserves more than this—their support. But he does not get it, and for the reason that, as things are now in Japan, the interests of the home manufacturer and those of the local trader are not identical. This is unfortunate, but it is none the less a fact.

As made clear in another chapter, I am not a great believer in the existence on a large scale of such a virtue as sentiment or gratitude in business. Did it exist in England, we should support our fellow-countrymen in Japan more than we do. But, alas! the British manufacturer wants to get orders; and, in practice, it turns out that he does not care where those orders come from as long as he receives them with a minimum of trouble and expense, and

INTERNATIONAL BUSINESS RELATIONS

provided he gets his money. From his point of view —a selfish one, no doubt—if he finds that a Japanese merchant firm gives him less trouble than a foreign firm, he prefers the former. And this is often the case, at all events, when it is a question of Government work; for the foreigners, in view of the complications with which the Japanese Government hedge round their contracts, very naturally try to exact strict guarantees from the manufacturers to protect themselves in some measure; whereas the Japanese merchant trusts somewhat to his luck, or to his diplomatic skill, or to special favoring from his own countrymen, whichever one likes to call it, to pull him through his difficulties with his Government.

All this falls very heavily on the foreign merchant in Japan, and it is not to be wondered at that he is pessimistic with regard to his position and prospects. Over and over again trading people in Yokohama, while complaining of the existing state of things, have told me that the coming into operation of the new treaties will be "the last straw" destined to break the back of their business, and that the effect will be that most of the long established and best known of these firms will leave the country.

How far this forecast is likely to hold good must of course be a matter of opinion. But if, as we are told, the days of the trading foreigner in Japan are numbered, it does not necessarily follow that the international business of the country will decline. Nor does it necessarily mean that business foreigners will not be needed in that country. The channels through which Japanese orders find their way to the manufacturer may be changed, and the orders may not in every case find their way to their present destinations. Consequently, it behooves manufacturers who wish to retain their Japanese trade to find out for themselves the best steps to be taken to secure that end.

Now the business foreigner of whom the Japanese are in want—although they do not, as a rule, acknowledge the fact—is the thoroughly technical man; and they want technical men in almost every capacity with regard to modern industrial concerns. They will not engage him and pay for him themselves, because, in their present ultra-nationalist frame of mind, they like to feel that they can do without him.

It may, however, pay some of our larger manufacturers to send over to Japan at their own expense men who thoroughly understand the details of their particular specialties, who will be in a position to tell the Japanese what they want to know. The ordinary commercial tout, whatever his value might have been in Japan years ago, is distinctly at a discount now. The Japanese business people have a good insight into modern business methods; they have their banking establishments all over the world, and they know how to make estimates and how to quote for most of the ordinary articles of commerce at the present day. But what they do not yet altogether know is how to select their makers of the foreign articles they require, and they are constantly

INTERNATIONAL BUSINESS RELATIONS

misled by the catalogues of inferior and even of bogus manufacturers. Again, they have not yet attained the industrial experience necessary to enable them to get the best results from such plant as they may purchase.

If, therefore, we are to assume that in course of time the native merchant will wipe out the local foreign merchant, who has stuck more to his home manufacturers than the home manufacturers have to him, the manufacturers will require to replace him by technical representatives, as above explained. Such men, if they are versed in all the details of the industries they represent, and, above all, if they run absolutely straight, will, by dint of educating the Japanese in that one branch of modern knowledge which they now neglect—the practical side of their industries as opposed to the theoretical—be able, if not to secure orders and do commercial business themselves, at all events to direct orders into the proper channels from their own and their employers' point of view.

To make my meaning quite clear as to the class of business man required in Japan at the present day, I would say that he should be one who, instead of trying to sell things to the Japanese, should pass his time in visiting factories where his machines or appliances were being used, and who could give practical advice to the Japanese users as to whether or not they had got the most suitable plant; and in putting them in the way of working such plant to the best advantage.

There are two considerations which are likely to make manufacturers hesitate before sending technical representatives of the above class to Japan. First, there are comparatively few firms who consider that the trade from that country would warrant the expenditure entailed by maintaining such a man—for he must be a good one—in Japan for considerable periods at a stretch. Secondly, it is obvious that when a good man of this sort has worked conscientiously for a long time among the Japanese, instructing them in the details of his particular industry at the expense of an individual firm, another such representative might come immediately after him, and from another firm, and reap much of the harvest for which his predecessor had sown the seeds. I see no other method, however, than the above for dealing satisfactorily with the Japanese in their present state of industrial knowledge.

The ordinary foreign commercial man is almost valueless at the present day, as an agent in Japan, for representing engineers, at all events; for he is not able to tell the Japanese any more than they know already; nor is an engineer of much good for the purpose unless he is more or less of a specialist with regard to the subjects he is dealing with.

It would be a different matter were the foreign agent to be able to deal directly with the native purchaser, but as a rule he is not; for he does not speak the language well enough, and consequently he has to negotiate either with the merchant firms or with big administrations, nearly all of which have commer-

INTERNATIONAL BUSINESS RELATIONS

cial and more or less technical people attached to them who possess a fair all-round knowledge of the subjects in question themselves. When such is the case, a foreigner, to do any good with them, must know at all events a little more of his subject than the man he is talking to. Many of the big foreign merchant firms are increasing the number of specialists on their staffs; but in the case of firms dealing in many varieties of articles, it is difficult to have a special man in each department. The treaty-port firms, too, are beginning to alter their policy somewhat to suit the times, and are rather less unbending in their attitude than they were in times gone by.

I cannot believe that the effect of the coming into force of the treaties, or the unjust handicapping of the foreigner above explained, or anything else, will knock out altogether such firms as may choose to adapt their policy to suit the new state of things. The local trader, more than any other section of the foreign community in Japan, has been the last to realize the enormous progress which has been going on. He it is who speaks less Japanese than any other section of the foreign community, and who associates less with the people of the country.

Years ago such exclusiveness was all very well; for then the Japanese if they wanted to buy anything from abroad had to apply to the treaty-port foreigner to get it for them. Now this is not only not necessary, but the Japanese merchants have, temporarily, at all events, been able to establish a serious and legal boycott injuriously affecting their foreign competitor, as explained earlier in this chapter.

It would be absurd to suggest that as time goes on the Japanese will become less capable of conducting their commercial transactions themselves; and, were it not for the fact that one may reasonably hope that the existing spirit of "down with the foreigner" cannot last forever, the future of the local foreign merchant would be bad indeed. If one applies, however, in a cold-blooded manner, the laws of economics to the question, one can only come to the conclusion either that in the long-run Japan will have to treat the foreigner on an ordinary, fair business basis, or she must come to grief, as far as her progressive policy is concerned. Quite apart from any question of war, the Powers whose business people she tries to hamper in her own country could in retaliation make matters so unpleasant for her as to stop her outward trade altogether, and at any time, if they felt inclined.

As stated above, the great stumbling-block to satisfactory trade with Japan is the want of knowledge of the Japanese language by our traders. Over and over again I have heard it said that it is quite useless to speak Japanese, because so many of them speak English. In fact, the Europeans who speak Japanese fluently seldom or never make use of it when talking to a Japanese who speaks their language even imperfectly, unless he is an intimate friend, as it is said that the Japanese resent the use of their language by a foreigner. But the fact remains that

INTERNATIONAL BUSINESS RELATIONS

the man who is not able to understand the language of the party he is dealing with is often at a very great disadvantage in carrying on an intricate negotiation.

In stating this I am aware that I am laying myself open to the criticism that to suggest that a knowledge of Japanese should be attained by our local traders is to suggest an impossibility. But, if this is so, it means that the Japanese must hold the whip-hand over the foreigner in commercial matters in their own country.

The British Government, which is not particularly noted for the break-neck speed with which it rushes ahead of the times, has long since grasped the fact that it is necessary that its local diplomatic and consular officials should speak Japanese, with the result that at the present day at least three of her Majesty's officials at Tokio, including the Minister, not only speak but read and write the language fluently. The life of the diplomatic students, too, who go out to Japan is made a burden for the first two years after their arrival, in wrestling with some of the complicated hieroglyphics out of the 80,000 which go to make up the ideographic system of the written language.

The business man will tell you, and possibly he is right, that life is not long enough to permit of an exhaustive study of Japanese. If that is so, it is to be feared that, from the moment that the Japanese have completed their modern education, the foreign trader, who once was placed on a pedestal, and who, if not liked, was, at all events, regarded with profound respect on account of his wonderful knowledge, will have lost all his prestige, and with it his chances of carrying on his business at a profit to himself.

If the days of the resident foreign commercial man are on the decline, those of the casual visiting commercial agent are in a no more satisfactory state. The local merchants, whether native or foreign, regard such men as interlopers, who wish to have the trade carried on in a different manner than according to the established local routine; as people, in fact, who are likely to disturb their business methods, and to do at the best but little good to trade. There is also, too, a lingering suspicion in the minds of the merchants that the new-comer is endeavoring to deal direct with the Japanese purchasers, and over their heads, or that his visit may eventually lead to such a policy being adopted.

My advice to manufacturers is not to attempt such a policy at the present day, but to direct their efforts rather towards urging their respective Governments to negotiate with the Government of Japan to treat the local foreign trader as fairly as Japanese traders are treated in Western countries.

CHAPTER X

MODERN INDUSTRIAL JAPAN

No more striking illustration of the wonderful adaptability of the Japanese character is to be found than that afforded by the readiness with which they have taken up Western methods of manufacturing.

Any one whose business it might be to visit the modern factories in the Japan of to-day, and who afterwards might pick up Rein's *Industries of Japan*, thoughtful and excellent in every way as is that work, might well imagine that what he had seen, and what he reads in that book, had to do with two absolutely different countries. This does not mean that the industrial Japan described so ably by Rein has ceased to exist, but that during the last few years, side by side with the picturesque, effective, and time-honored native handicrafts, there have sprung into being the essentially progressive, but inartistic factory chimney and its accompanying and still more hideous workshops, built on the most approved of European and American designs.

My advice to the visitor to Japan who wishes to enjoy himself and improve his mind is to study the industrial Japan depicted by Rein; for, though less obtrusive, it still remains, and is far more interesting than its modern congener. Let him see the making of cloisonné-ware, embroidery, rice-mats, and carving, and admire the curios, toys, hand-weaving, and painting, while these arts are still to be seen as now carried on; for my conviction is that if the old Japan is destined to die, as we are so often told is to be the case, mortification will first attack its native industries.

To acquire the necessary efficiency in these old crafts demanded a life-long application, commencing at an early age—that is to say, at a period of life which has now to be devoted to more modern and general education. Such work insured to the 'prentice hand, and even to the full-blown workman, a remuneration so small as to be quite inadequate to meet what will be considered as the necessities of life to the Japanese of the coming generation.

The modern factory has had the effect of trebling the wages of the Japanese artisan in three years, and under such circumstances it is hardly likely that the working classes of to-day will be able to afford to stick to their old arts and industries at the old prices. For the modern factory-owner is there to offer a very high rate of wages on the condition that these naturally clean people shall come and dirty themselves for a certain number of hours every day in his workshops.

The only thing which has tended to save the situation in some degree up till now is the fact that the artistic instincts of the Japanese revolt against the factory system, the effect of which is to convert the man into a machine—that is to say, to make him work without intelligence and without responsibility, according to the ideal of the modern trade-union. For every Japanese workman is by instinct an artist as well as an artisan, and consequently it has been his wont to throw his individuality into his work. This it is that has lent the artistic charm to a paper and bamboo fan costing less than a half-penny, or to the Japanese doll we find in Christmas crackers sold to us for a few pence per dozen.

Most people who write about China tell their readers at some stage or other that the Chinese are so conscientious in imitating a given article that if you were to send a tailor a suit of clothes to copy, and there happened to be a tear somewhere, he would faithfully reproduce the tear in making the new suit. With the Japanese workmen the situation is reversed; for if you tell a carpenter to make even a plain wooden box exactly like a sample, the chances are that the new one will vary in some manner from the original. The difference may or may not be an improvement, but it will be there. Thus it is that the Chinese make better factory hands than the Japanese.

It is owing to the tendency of the Japanese artisan to remain faithful to his native arts and industries that, in order to get factory hands in sufficient numbers, the owners have had to lift wages to the large extent mentioned above, and thus it is, as time goes on and the growing generation gets habituated to the factory, the artistic capabilities, of the lower class Japanese, at all events, will be crushed out of him by the steam-hammer and the hydraulic press.

He will become demoralized as an artist and as a man, but he will have gained in "civilization" and importance. He will have become an enlightened member of society, capable of reading his anti-capitalist newspapers, and of more or less understanding politics; he will have acquired greatly increased wants, and yet be in a position to pay considerable sums in support of a trade-union worked on the most approved of modern systems.

Certain writers have from time to time pointed out the small remuneration which has been meted out to the Japanese workman, and have used the figures somewhat unfairly for the purpose of showing how down-trodden and unfortunate were the workers in Japan as compared with those in their own country. I can only say that I have not found —even among the extremely poor in Japan—a tithe of the misery and degradation to be met with in the course of an ordinary walk through the streets of London or New York, or in any of the big Continental capitals.

In Osaka and other big manufacturing centres the accumulating factories are beginning to inaugurate something of this sort of degradation of living which usually accompanies prosperous modern industries elsewhere; but up to the present the life of the working people of Japan has not become sufficiently modernized to compare either in dirt or misery with that of our lowest classes. No doubt,

H.I.H. THE LATE PRINCE SANJO
First Premier after the Restoration

VISCOUNT YENOMOTO
Formerly Minister of Agriculture and Commerce

however, industrial progress will effect this in time.

The Japanese, when once they decided to make their country a modern one, took the industrial bull by the horns, and began by building railways.

The Emperor formally sanctioned their introduction in 1869, under extremely urgent pressure from certain progressive statesmen.

In almost every country the introduction of railways has met with violent opposition from a large and powerful section of the community, and Japan was no exception to this rule.

Among the men whose names are now familiar as champions of Japanese progress are some, strange to say, who were at the time the most persistent in their opposition to the introduction of railways. However, when the Emperor had been gained over to sanction them, this opposition was overpowered, and their construction was at once proceeded with.

Not very far short of two hundred foreigners, in all capacities, were engaged by the Japanese Government to organize and build the first lines. By the time, however, that about one hundred and fifty miles had been constructed less than twenty foreigners remained on the staff.

To-day, with over 3000 miles of lines in the four islands of Hondo, Kyushu, Shikoku, and Hokkaido, there are only three foreigners left in the employ of the Imperial Japanese Railways.

At first, with that wonderful forethought which characterizes the organization of nearly all the big projects of the Japanese, the Government took on itself the whole responsibility of construction and running. But when it was considered that the Japanese engineers and business people had learned enough of the details of railway working and management for private companies to be able to run them, the Government granted, in 1881, a tentative and very liberal charter to the Japan Railway Company, and, in order to insure the thing being done properly, undertook the construction and working of the lines for that company for a period of ten years.

Since then a great number of charters have been granted on decreasingly liberal terms, until at the present day some forty railway companies control the entire system, the Imperial Railways representing about one-third of the total mileage.

The captious critic has an easy field for finding a great deal of fault with regard to the conditions under which these railways are maintained and run from a Western point of view; but if we bear in mind that they were built to meet Japanese requirements and not European, there is little to be said against them; and when we take into consideration the extreme difficulties which confront the railway engineer in Japan, in the shape of mountainous country, earthquakes, and floods, with their attendant evils, one can only admire extremely the skill and patience of both the foreign and native organizers of this now big and effective railway system.

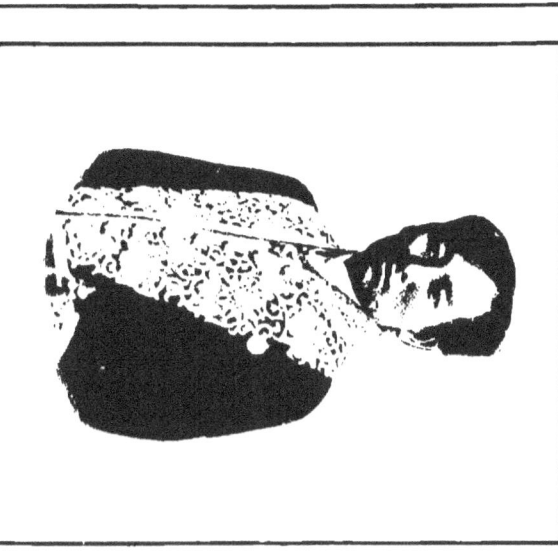

BARON ITO
Formerly Minister of Agriculture and Commerce

BARON NISHI
For many years Japanese Minister in St. Petersburg, and afterwards Minister of Foreign Affairs in Japan

Simultaneously with the building of railways, Japan began to create a modern mercantile marine, and the Government has logically followed out its policy by fostering this in a proportionately liberal manner.

As Nature has provided the "permanent-way" for ships, the Government did not find it necessary to run their own merchant vessels, and they therefore contented themselves with judiciously subsidizing not only the private capitalists who ran steamers but the native ship-builders who had enterprise enough to begin building them.

This policy of the Government of nursing the railways and mercantile fleet in a manner which entailed very great expense has been much criticised; and it has over and over again been said that the Japanese, in their state of vainglorious inflation, were trying to do too much, and that in the end they must come to lamentable grief; but I can see no reason for such a theory as far as railways and steamships are concerned, for these may be described as the necessary arteries of modern commerce, and without them the Japanese could not hope to succeed in the industrial struggle for life.

The proof, too, of the pudding is in the eating, to use a vulgar expression, and the railways, at all events, have proved a great financial success. In fact, I do not think that there is any complete railway system of 3000 miles in the world which has been worked to so great a profit per mile as that of Japan. The carping critic is also very fond of pointing out that many of the smaller companies are in a very rotten condition, and so they are; but as fast as they become so they are absorbed into the larger ones, and in the long-run go to add to the general industrial strength of Japan.

With regard to the shipping subsidies, the Government are no doubt still very much out of pocket by their enterprise, but everything points to the conclusion that with patience and perseverance in their present policy they will eventually have created not only a very powerful, but an extremely profitable mercantile marine as a permanent benefit to the trade of their country.

In the solution of the modern industrial problem in the country, the feature that strikes one most forcibly is that, while in countries like Russia, Spain, Portugal, Italy, Turkey, Greece, Mexico, and the South American Republics, to say nothing of China and India, in all of which the labor in the engineering and other "skilled" trades can often be satisfactorily drilled into shape from native material, the heads of departments and the active technical chiefs are very often foreigners — usually Englishmen, Americans, or Germans; in Japan this is not so.

Except in certain industrial concerns in the treaty-ports, owned by foreigners, there is hardly such a thing as an executive foreigner at the head of any Japanese factory or administration.

A German or two will be found managing a brewery, and a few Scotchmen in ship-building yards, and so on; and that is all. You can visit

SHIMBASHI RAILWAY STATION, TOKIO

The chief terminus of the imperial railways. This station was built when there were only eighteen miles of railway in Japan. At the present day there are about three thousand.

MITSU BISHI BANK

MODERN INDUSTRIAL JAPAN

arsenals and dockyards, and nearly all the railway and engineering shops, and you will see no sign of a foreigner anywhere. You will be received in a foreign office by people in foreign clothes, with all the paraphernalia of foreign business around them. You will be talked to in English, as a rule, and you will be shown through works built on English lines, and filled with workmen dressed like English mechanics, working at English vices or at machines with the names of English makers on them. But you are the only Englishman or European there, and you look around and ask yourself how it has all been done.

Your Japanese friend does not tell you of any foreign assistance, though you see the hand of the foreigner in all. But where is he? And your thoughts instinctively revert back to the great educational establishments of Japan, more particularly to the scientific branches of the Imperial Tokio University, and to the small bevy of quiet, unassuming men who foregather at the little Tokio Club, the foreign advisers still left in the various branches of the Japanese service. Then it is that you realize, for the first time to its full extent, the colossal nature of the work carried out by these men, and by those who have gone; men who have given their best energies and the best part of their lives to bringing about the enlightened Japan of to-day; and you have reason to feel proud that many of them are countrymen of your own. For while the foreigner is no longer executive, and, in fact, in most cases has disappeared, the influence of the work he has carried out so thoroughly and so well is apparent throughout modern industrial Japan.

It would, of course, be better for the Japanese had they retained the foreigner rather longer as an active director in their factories, for signs are visible everywhere that, in many cases, they have not yet mastered all the practical details of the work they are carrying out. The Japanese have among them many capable engineers and technical men, but their thoroughly skilled labor, in many branches, is, and must be for many years to come, very defective in quality and quantity; and at the present stage it is more the practical foreman, who can personally instruct the common laborer, than the theoretical man who is required.

The weak point in the Japanese industrial world, apart from the limited amount of skilled labor available, is to be found in the fact that the practical side of the training of the highly educated man has been more neglected than any other.

In England, when a young man leaves his technical college we look on him as having only just gone through the first portion of his training as an engineer, electrician, or architect, after which he is expected to face the practical drudgery of the workshops or drawing-office, as the case may be. The Japanese have not yet grasped the fact that it is in no sense a degradation for the man who has paid for an education which has enabled him to master the theory to dirty his hands in acquiring the practice.

But until they understand this, the Japanese will never work their factories to the best advantage, as the heads of departments will never fully know their business. They will come to realize this fact later on, when the Tokio University and kindred institutions have had time to turn out a sufficient number of graduates to glut the professional market.

At the present time, the demand is greater than the supply, and any one, on leaving college, can find himself in an excellent situation. But this state of things will not last very much longer.

Wonderful as has been the progress of the Japanese in manufacturing by modern means, the state of perfection at which they have arrived has often been grossly exaggerated. They have done much, very much more than it was anticipated that they could possibly have accomplished in so short a time, but those alarmists who talk about the Japanese being able to oust us from the world's markets are speaking without their book, and without any knowledge of economics. Such people have usually based their argument on the assumption that Japanese wages are still so low that, when they have become as efficient as we are, they will make it impossible for us to compete with them.

This would be all very well, if there were a law in Japan that for the next fifty years wages were not to be raised above their present scale, but as no country could enforce such a law, and Japanese wages are going up by leaps and bounds, and in the natural course of things must continue to do so as time goes on, the argument does not hold good.

There is another item to be reckoned with in studying the economics of Japanese manufacturing, and that is that many of the materials employed in their modern industries are much more expensive to purchase there than in various other countries. Now, as the Japanese Government have fallen into the error of adopting a rising protective tariff on imported goods, the cost of materials stands a good chance of being enhanced simultaneously with the price of labor.

Thus, with regard to most of our industries, we may rest assured that we shall not be seriously threatened for many years to come; and we may, at least in our skilled trades, look on the Japanese industrial advance, not only with interest, but with competitive complacency as far as our markets in other countries are concerned.

Among the modern industries worked on modern lines which the Japanese may be said to have mastered in a manner which would enable them to compete internationally, the following trades can be mentioned: coal-mining, cotton and other spinning, printing, type-founding, engraving, photography, instrument-making, boot, clothes, and match making, brewing, bread-making, and certain branches of electrical work.

I look on the Japanese, too, as being good railway engineers in many respects, though there is a great diversity of opinion on that point. As manufacturing engineers they are not yet by any means proficient on any large scale, and I do not think I am going too far in saying that there has never been made in Japan, as a commercial success, such a thing as a purely Japanese steam-engine.

It is true they have made a few extremely good locomotives, and these are almost the most difficult type of engine to be made by beginners. I am told, too, that these engines came out advantageously with regard to cost price as compared with similar ones imported from abroad. But while the construction of such engines reflected the greatest credit on the Japanese, one must not forget that they were turned out under the direct supervision and from the detailed designs of an English locomotive superintendent.

Of modern ships of from 1000 to 4000 tons, both for the navy and mercantile marine, they have made many, sometimes under European control and sometimes without it, and such ships have been good in quality; but most of the intricate mechanism in their construction was imported, and from a commercial point of view they have worked out much more expensively than would have been the case had they been purchased from abroad.

Their largest effort in this way was the *Hitachi Maru*, launched at Nagasaki last year, the registered capacity of which was 6150 tons.

In engineering and ship-building, however, great progress is being made, and although the Japanese may just now be debiting heavy losses to their inexperience account, there is no doubt that the improvement which will come with time will lead to Japan some day being a large engineering centre.

Small-arms, and all that appertains thereto, are satisfactorily made entirely under Japanese control at the arsenals. They have not yet, however, succeeded in turning out large ordnance as efficiently as it is done in China, at the Kiangnan Arsenal, near Shanghai.

I saw in a recent book by a well-known authority that there were many "steel foundries" in Japan, but I can only say that I failed to find them. One large steel-works, at all events, is in the process of being started, but the Japanese until now even as iron founders, on modern lines, have not been very successful.

Wood-working by machinery, except for railway carriage and wagon work, they have only just commenced on any large scale, and they have not yet mastered the intricacies of the trade. Although Japan is distinctly a timber country, she has until lately neglected this department of modern industry; and this is doubtless due in a great measure to the fact that, as hand-workers in wood, the Japanese are the most skilful operators in the world.

The building up of iron and steel structures, such as bridges, turn-tables, and boilers, from imported girders and plates is very creditably carried on; and in constructing what are known as "earthquake-

THE NAGASAKI SHIP-BUILDING WORKS

proof" chimneys made of sheet steel lined with brick, and sometimes 200 feet high, they are very skilful.

It is well to point out here an interesting similarity between the evolution of the industrial problem in Japan and in Great Britain, which should go some way to prove that circumstances have decided that the destiny of that country is to be worked out on British lines.

Years ago, one may almost say centuries ago, the preponderating industry of Great Britain was agriculture. Long since, however, we have given up seriously endeavoring to feed ourselves, and have found it policy to allow our agriculture to go to the wall, confining our industrial policy to manufacturing only those products which afforded us the greatest profit. With the money thus obtained we have purchased most of our food from foreign countries and our colonies.

Japan, too, has been essentially an agricultural country, but now on a rapidly declining scale. Perhaps it would be more accurate to say that year by year her increased modern industries are absorbing the labor available for agricultural purposes, and the value of manufactured products is gradually assuming the upper hand.

Agriculture still slightly preponderates over the manufactured products, but I believe at the present day the proportion is only as fifty-five to forty-five, whereas a few years ago agriculture was a very long way ahead.

JAPAN IN TRANSITION

Japan is now importing her staple-food commodity—rice—as England imports her corn.

The modern industries of Japan are now dotting themselves about all over the country. The greatest centre of these industries is undoubtedly Osaka; omitting of course Tokio, which, as a city, is vastly more extended, and in which, consequently, the factories, being spread over a far greater area, are not so self-evident. Tokio, at all events, pulls the industrial strings in Japan.

Osaka now may be said to be fast developing into an industrial city pure and simple; and this is no doubt why I have heard Englishmen call it the Manchester, and Scotchmen the Glasgow, and Frenchmen the Lille, and Germans the Hamburg, and Americans the Chicago, of Japan.

One sees of course the idea which gave birth to these respective similes; and yet Osaka is not in the least like any one of the cities mentioned, and never will be; for the individuality of the Japanese will always be strong enough to prevent the possibility of their adopting any of our Western methods in their entirety, even in the carrying out of their modern industries.

CHAPTER XI

THE EFFECT OF THE WAR ON FOREIGN RELATIONS

It is not necessary for me to dwell on the condition of the Japanese before their war with China, beyond recalling the fact that for years previous to that event —that is to say, ever since the abolition of the Shogunate—they had been absorbing Western education, and adopting such of our modern methods as they thought desirable, at a rate which would have taken away our breath had we realized its extent at the time.

Speaking generally, however, the outside world had no idea that the progress which was being made by the Japanese was of a genuine nature. It is true that we heard that they were buying many things, endeavoring to copy our inventions, and generally burlesquing our methods. I should, of course, be plagiarizing every writer who had touched on Japan during the last five years if I were to say that the Chino-Japanese war opened the eyes of the foreigner to the fact that, at all events as far as strategy was concerned, the Japanese had really profited by their studies.

The complete and overwhelming success of the Japanese, however, came as such a shock to the average foreigner that he has been wont to date the progress of Japan from that time only, and to ignore the steady and conscientious educational "grind" which the people of that country had been undergoing at the hands of their European and American instructors quietly and unostentatiously for the five-and-twenty years which preceded that event.

We are told that before the war the Japanese were diffident, gentle, and courteous to the foreigner, that they recognized his superiority, and so on. Now it is said that at the present day they have lost all these qualities, and that they are bumptious and self-assertive. The fact of the matter is that, until the war took place, the Japanese had not had an opportunity of demonstrating either to themselves or to the world in general the headway they had made. In fact, it has been maintained by some that the war was in a great measure brought about for the purpose of making a practical demonstration of the sort. However this may be, it only stands to reason that their self-confidence, which had always been a strong, if a dormant, element in the Japanese character, should become emphasized, or, at all events, be much more in evidence than was the case before the war.

But, as victorious countries go, Japan behaved, even immediately after the war, with wonderful clear-headedness and tact. Excesses she may have committed — excesses of exuberance, excesses of speech, and excesses of expenditure — but she did not lose her head, and, on the whole, her behavior after her victory was exemplary.

It has been my lot to be in several countries

H.I.H. THE LATE PRINCE ARISUGAWA
Chief of the General Staff. Died during the war with China
Photographed by OGAWA

EFFECT OF WAR ON FOREIGN RELATIONS

shortly after wars, revolutions, and political upheavals of one sort or another had taken place, and I can only say that I have never known a victorious people to take their successes so modestly as have the Japanese.

Among the more important, and certainly the least noticed, effects which the war produced on Japan, was the turn it gave to Japanese party-political organization. It is not necessary to emphasize this here, as the subject is more fully dealt with in the chapter on "Politics in the Past and Present." I would, however, mention in passing that the patriotic wave of feeling which passed over the country at the time completely swamped the hitherto increasingly antagonistic feelings of the many political groups, which were threatening the existence of modern government in Japan, and brought all politicians into one camp for the time being.

That Russia, France, and Germany committed a gross act of injustice to Japan in combining to fetter her action in China at the close of the war, and to rob her to a great extent of the legitimate spoils of her victory, goes without saying. England has cause to be thankful that she did not aid and abet that unholy triple alliance. Not only was the combined action of those Powers unjust to Japan, but it was detrimental to the interests of civilization; for Japanese political influence at Peking just then would have been the most healthy and efficacious tonic that could possibly have been administered to the sick Chinaman.

JAPAN IN TRANSITION

It has been proved past argument that Russian influence in the Far East is not of a civilizing nature. Should any one wish to compare the Russian and Japanese methods of civilization, let him study on the one hand the Russian administration in the island of Saghalien, from which the Japanese were ousted in 1875 by "treaty," and on the other the Japanese administration in the neighboring islands. Let him compare the Russian convict prisons in Saghalien with the Japanese prisons in Tokio. Let him compare the methods of the Russians at Inasa (near Nagasaki), which is to all intents and purposes a Russian concession, with those of the Japanese in any part of their own country. Let him compare the primeval and degrading galley-slave system in vogue on the Russian men-of-war with the Japanese naval discipline.

Whatever may have been the immediate effect of the Franco-Germano-Russian action in checking Japanese influence, there can be no doubt that in the long-run Japan will play a strong, if not a preponderating, part in the civilizing of China; for the Japanese understand the Chinese character a great deal better than is the case with the people of any other nation, and they have facilities in the way of possessing a practically identical written language, a knowledge of which Westerners as a class cannot hope to attain. In addition to this there exists between Japan and China a racial sympathy.

When once China has been really civilized, it is not probable that either Japan or any other nation

EFFECT OF WAR ON FOREIGN RELATIONS

will have a great deal of influence with her; but it is reasonable to suppose that as soon as that process has been accomplished China and Japan will be found on the same side when it is a question of facing a common Western enemy. That date, however, is still so far distant that it would be futile to speculate as to its probable effect now, or to do more than point out in passing that an eventual alliance with China in the dim future is the avowed dream of Japanese politicians of to-day.

Although the Japanese appear to have just now an undue contempt for the Chinese, and for Chinese methods, there is no real deep-rooted hatred of the Chinaman. There is none of that feeling of violent animosity such as exists, for instance, between France and Germany, Germany and Denmark, Greece and Turkey, or Russia and Finland.

One of the most satisfactory effects of the war has been that it has caused the Japanese to discriminate between foreigners to some extent; for until then, in the same ignorant way in which the average Westerner was wont to look on a Japanese as being a sort of Chinaman without a pigtail, so the Japanese looked upon most Europeans and Americans as being a sort of Englishmen.

As Englishmen, because there were more Englishmen than other Western foreigners in Japan, because English was the language which all local foreigners had to speak, because England was the country with which most international commerce was carried on, and because the Japanese saw more

English ships than those of all other nations put together.

The power of discriminating between the Western races, which has of late years come to the Japanese, has been, on the whole, greatly to the advantage of the Anglo-Saxon.

In a general way the Japanese regarded the Western foreigner as a rough, rude, dictatorial, and immoral man, with a long nose and having hair all over his face; who was always making a noise, and was addicted to intemperate habits. He had, however, the redeeming features of being very rich, and of possessing a wonderful store of knowledge on a variety of subjects, which, when mastered, would be invaluable to the Japanese. In conversing with uneducated Japanese it will be found that the same impression holds good very much at the present day. Grotesque as such an estimate of our personal attractions may seem to us, it is no more so than some of the impressions we have held of the Japanese; and when one bears in mind the fact that our appearance is so different from theirs, that the manners of our most gentlemanly and considerate people appear abrupt to them, and that they have based their ideas of us on the roughest and noisiest section of the foreign community, we must admit that their appreciation of our individuality, however unflattering and inaccurate, is at least intelligible.

International politics and trade, the dissensions among the local missionaries, and especially the different attitudes adopted by the various Powers at

THE MARQUIS ITO

Photographed by OGAWA

EFFECT OF WAR ON FOREIGN RELATIONS

the time of the war with China, have caused the educated classes to discover the fact that there are foreigners and foreigners. And among these foreigners for the last year or two the Anglo-Saxons, if not liked better, are at all events more respected than the rest, as explained above. The reason for this is, not that our manners are, from the Japanese point of view, better than those of other foreigners, for as a matter of fact they often consider us more exacting and dictatorial than the others, but because they are beginning to realize more and more that, as far as modern institutions go, their methods must be based on our methods. They find that in the longrun their trade with Great Britain and America runs more smoothly than with other countries, and they know more where they are when dealing with us than they do with our Continental brethren. They find also that, if we do not make many social or business concessions to them, we at all events do not bother them in their politics, and, above all, we do not use our diplomatic organization as a sort of commercial agency to force trade into British channels.

The comparative popularity of Great Britain with the Japanese, dates, of course, more particularly, from the close of the war. Very little distinction is still made between Americans and Englishmen in the minds of the Japanese, and incidentally the Anglo-Saxon owes much of his present popularity to the American branch of that race, for the Americans have, as a rule, been more intimate with the Japanese, and in dealing with them have been less unbending in their attitude than we have.

For a short period in 1897, when the Hawaiian question was first on the *tapis*, the Japanese expressed a great deal of resentment against the United States, but this was mainly due to the fact that America did not show a great deal of political tact in dealing with the question; and, although Japan had never any serious wish to annex the islands, she no doubt resented very much some of the expressions made use of by politicians in Washington with regard to herself. At about the same time, a very material rise in the American tariff, with regard to certain articles which directly and very seriously affected Japanese exports to that country, added fuel to the resentment against the United States, but such resentment was not very long-lived.

Germany's influence in Japan, which during the Bismarck era was strong—so strong, in fact, that a portion of the railways were built by Germans on the German system, and even Japanese women made a trial of discarding their picturesque costume in favor of the most hideous ready-made apparel imported from the Fatherland—is on the decline. In fact, the railway in question has been reorganized, and is now worked on the British principle, and the ladies have reverted to their national dress.

And yet it would seem that the Germans are doing a thriving trade with Japan; and, if we are to believe the consular statistics, their trade is increasing. But figures are strange things to deal in, and, when

EFFECT OF WAR ON FOREIGN RELATIONS

studying the German trade reports, we have to face the complications caused by the fact that, in order to make both ends meet at all, most of the local German traders have to handle British goods; and not only this, but they have to pass off much of their native produce as being of British make, even when to do so the goods in question have to be shipped from England.

The Latin races are not numerous in Japan, and their influence is almost *nil* at the present day, except that, if any Christian missionaries can be said to make headway at all among the Japanese, they are the French Jesuits.

The Dutch, who centuries ago were the most powerful of all foreigners in Japan, and used their power to have other foreigners massacred, are no longer to be reckoned with at all.

Russia, of course, as a nation, is cordially detested by the Japanese, although Russian residents are on good enough terms with the people. There is always, however, a lingering thought in the minds of the Japanese that a Russian visitor is a spy; for, as a Japanese friend of mine put it, who had himself seen the inside of a Russian prison for making some sketches of fortifications in that country, "the Russians have no business interests in Japan, and it cannot pay them to come and live here for the purposes of business."

Russian methods do not in any possible way appeal to the Japanese, and, although Russia is Japan's nearest neighbor, the Japanese assimilate less of

Russia in their process of modernizing their country than of any other nation. And yet Russia's influence is directly and powerfully felt, for had it not been the fixed conviction that Russia was the natural and persistent enemy of Japan the latter Power would not have seen the necessity of developing her defensive equipment to anything like the extent she has done in so short a time.

I have often heard it said that since the war, and especially during the last two years, Japan has been "spoiling for a fight"; that it did not much matter who the enemy might be, but that she was consumed with an ardent desire to "have a go for" somebody or other. I am bound to say that during the time I was living in Japan I never saw any sign of the sort of feverish unrest which usually characterizes a nation imbued with that idea. No doubt, if England had seen fit to suggest a hostile co-operation against Russian aggression in China at the beginning of last year (1898), Japan would have cordially fallen in with such a measure. There are no doubt many who might have criticised her policy had she done so, but she would not have been acting in a reckless manner. She would have been following out a line of action which she hoped might afford a means towards the end which she had mapped out for herself in the future.

Japan's ambition is eventually to hold the same position in Eastern Asia as England does in Western Europe; and to effect this will be the beginning and the end of Japanese foreign policy for many

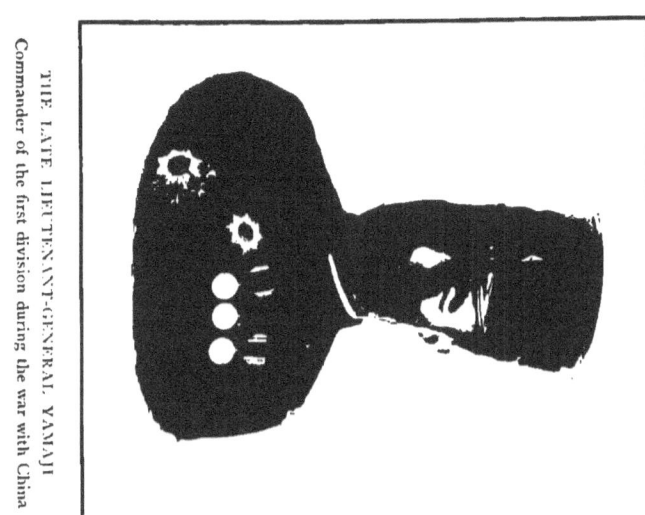

THE LATE LIEUTENANT-GENERAL YAMAJI
Commander of the first division during the war with China

COUNT ITAGAKI
The organizer and leader of the *Jiyu-Ta* or "Liberal Party"

years to come. In Russia she recognizes the Power who is more likely than all the others to put obstacles in her path, and, from the Japanese point of view, it is Russia whose action should be thwarted. Those nations, therefore, whose interests are at the greatest degree of divergence from those of Russia are consequently, for the time being, Japan's greatest friends.

I have not endeavored to enumerate in detail here all the effects that the war with China has had on Japan, as many of these become self-evident in the subjects dealt with in other chapters. To sum the matter up, however, the grand result of it has been that the official seal of approval has been placed by the nations of the world on the fact that Japan was to be reckoned with as a Power who, within measurable time, would have a right to be considered as one of the civilized nations of the world.

After the victory over the Chinese by force of arms, Japan scored a diplomatic victory over the civilized world by successfully applying for a revision of her treaties with foreign Powers; and Great Britain may congratulate herself as having been the first of these to accede to Japan's request. If, on the one hand, we may congratulate ourselves on having done so, we have every reason, on the other, to blame ourselves for the slipshod manner in which we did it. For, as explained in the chapter on "Our Prospects Under the Revised Treaties," the interests of our fellow-countrymen in Japan were not properly studied in the contract we made with Japan, as signed by Lord Kimberley. In fact, we have to thank other countries, who subsequently effected treaties with Japan, for such redeeming features as the last of them contained in favor of the foreigner. And we can safely say that had some country other than Great Britain taken the initiative with regard to treaty revision, the position of the foreigner in Japan would be better than it is to-day; for we should have realized the weak points in the treaties of the other Powers, and should have taken some trouble to insist on certain modifications when our turn came.

CHAPTER XII

POLITICS IN THE PAST AND PRESENT

JAPANESE internal politics in their present form are so kaleidoscopic that I shall not endeavor to do more than sketch a general outline of the manner in which the country is governed at the present time under the Constitutional régime. Were I to particularize in detail the different political cliques, with their varying shades of opinion, or were I to name a great number of the statesmen beyond those who stand out in a striking manner, the reader would be hopelessly confused; and, what is worse, any remarks I might make would very soon be out of date.

The ephemeral nature of Japanese political news was impressed on me most vividly when I had occasion to send articles from Tokio on that subject to a London paper. Writing under such conditions, the foreign correspondent in that part of the world does not see his handiwork in print for at least three months after it has been written and despatched to London; and on more than one occasion, in perusing my political articles after a lapse of twelve or fourteen weeks, I experienced the unpleasant sensation of finding that what I was reading had been deprived of its point by later events.

Again, I find that though barely a year has elapsed since I left Japan, the names are cropping up of politicians who, if known locally during my time, had given up till then but little proof of their capacity. Some of these will doubtless make a lasting name for themselves, but most of them are merely here to-day and will be gone to-morrow, and of such it is as well not to write; for, under these conditions, anything more than an outline study of the details of party politics in Japan could be of but little interest.

Looking back to an article I wrote from Tokio in November, 1896, I find I said:

"One of the most important effects of the war between China and Japan has been the simplifying of Japanese politics. In this respects, at all events, the war has proved itself an unmixed blessing to this country, in drawing together the very numerous political cliques, which were daily increasing in number and in bitterness of feeling against each other. Had it not been for the outburst of patriotic enthusiasm which swept Japan at that time, nothing could have amalgamated these small opposing parties, whose actions were rapidly bringing about so complicated a political tangle that a dead-lock must have shortly ensued."

This was perfectly true at the time; and, as a record of events, is perfectly true now. But whereas in 1896 and 1897 there was a distinct reason for going into that question, it has lost much of its point now. At that time "the outburst of patriotic

POLITICS PAST AND PRESENT

enthusiasm" referred to, occasioned by the war of 1894, still made itself felt in the Japanese political world, and held contending parties more or less together; whereas, at the present day, the strength of that wave of feeling has spent itself.

Japan has had to draw in her financial horns, and unanimity of political feeling has disappeared. It is not that the Japanese are less patriotic now than they were, but the enthusiasm which necessarily follows a successful war has in a great measure subsided; and, in measure as it has done so, the petty jealousies of party politicians, effectually smothered for the time being, have emerged from their hiding-places and resumed their activity. Thus it is that just now political cliques are as numerous and as diversified in their views as they were before the war.

Before dealing with politics as they are, it is as well to run over briefly the facts that led up to the present state of things; and in criticising Japanese methods of the present day, we must not lose sight of the extraordinary fact that in less than thirty years Japan has run through all the political phases which lie between feudalism of the most uncompromising order and a Constitutional Government on modern principles.

It would have been too much to expect that so rapid and extensive a series of transformations could have been effected without entailing grave political errors, and delicate situations of many sorts. But the most remarkable feature of it all is that during the whole of the period in question only one really serious internal conflict took place—viz., the Satsuma Rebellion in 1877.

On the subject of this terrible struggle, which took the form of a revolt of the most powerful clan in Japan against the modernizing influences which were at work in the country, and an endeavor to reinstate the old order of things, it is only necessary to say that it was eventually suppressed, and its suppression drove home the last nail in the coffin of Japanese feudalism.

One of the features which marked what is generally known in Japan as the Restoration — that is to say, the abolition of the Shogunate, in 1867—was an oath taken by the Mikado, on the occasion of his becoming vested once more with absolute power, to the effect that a popular Diet should be established in Japan.

The procrastination in giving effect to the promise conveyed by this oath, and the differences of opinion as to the actual meaning to be conveyed by it, eventually led to, or at all events afforded an excuse for, very serious political complications.

After the abolition of the Shogunate the Government had passed into the hands of the Samurai, who, while still belonging to the better classes, and possessing in some measure old-time instincts, were more enterprising and enlightened than their predecessors, and whose programme embraced from the first the modernizing of Japan. Things began to go too fast, however, for certain of the members of the

POLITICS PAST AND PRESENT

Cabinet, who were strongly anti-foreign in their feelings, and eventually their antagonism to the progressive policy brought about the Satsuma Rebellion.

But, previously to this, serious dissensions had arisen in the Ministry between the Progressists themselves. In the opinion of some politicians, the reforms were not sufficiently sweeping or rapid. This led to Count Itagaki, who may be described as the first real Radical in Japan, and certain of his followers separating themselves from their colleagues, and forming a party of malcontents on their own account. This group of politicians has now developed into one of the great contending parties of the present day, the *Juyu-to*, or " Liberal Party."

This was the first split in the Cabinet, and took place in 1873, and although prompt measures were taken for the suppression of Count Itagaki's followers, by imprisonment and banishment, and although at that time the policy of these ultra-radicals was destructive only, the party thrived and attained considerable moral influence, though entirely devoid of actual power. The strong individuality and honesty of purpose of Count Itagaki, whose political enemies did not accuse him of being anything worse than a dangerously progressive man, were sufficiently weighty to out-balance the amount of discredit from which his party suffered on account of the actions of some hangers-on of doubtful reputation.

In 1881, however, another split occurred in the Cabinet, the leading dissentient being Count

Okuma. His party adopted the policy of insisting on the establishing of a popular Diet, maintaining that the Mikado's oath of 1867 clearly promised that such an institution should be forthcoming, and that the time had now arrived for its realization. This party, known as the *Kaishin-to*, or " Party of Progress," was in many ways as radical in its leanings as the original " Party of Liberty "; but although in a great measure the aims of these two bodies were identical, they were absolutely hostile to each other in their working. This was mainly due to the fact that the individual ambitions of the leaders would not allow these gentlemen to make concessions to a rival political party.

In fighting his battle with the Government, however, Count Okuma overrated his strength, with the result that he had to retire from the Cabinet, in which he then held the position of Minister of Finance. Many followed him, and thus three distinct parties were in existence in 1882—viz., the Government, at the head of which were Marquis Ito and Count Inouye; the " Party of Progress," with Count Okuma; and the " Party of Liberty," with Count Itagaki, as their respective leaders.

But while these two latter parties were at daggers drawn with each other, their combined moral power, which was always in antagonism to the Government, was so great that it sufficed to wring from the Emperor a rescript to the effect that a Diet should be formed, not immediately, but in 1890. In due time the Diet was constituted, and took the form of a

COUNT INOUYE

POLITICS PAST AND PRESENT

Lower House, all the members of which were, nominally at all events, elected by popular vote; and an Upper House, some members of which sat by right of nobility, while others were nominated by the Emperor, and others by certain large taxpayers.

Ministers, however, had nothing whatever to do with either House, although they had the right of speaking but not of voting. They were responsible only to the Emperor, and could, if they thought it advisable, ignore the Diet completely. Hitherto the masses in Japan had taken no interest whatever in politics, and at the present day the amount of interest taken by them is very small compared with the political fever which rages among the lower classes in more advanced countries.

But even the moneyed, industrial, and commercial classes had had no part, active or otherwise, in framing the laws or influencing the policy of their country previously to the forming of the Parliament. The immediate effect of the new Constitution was that the Lower House at once became thronged in tolerably equal measure with partisans of the "Party of Liberty" and the "Party of Progress"; while the Government, beneath whose dignity it was to canvass, was left out in the cold.

The following table serves to show the relative proportions of the various classes of society who went to make up the members of the Imperial Diet from 1890, the first year, until 1897, the eighth year of the Constitutional regime:

JAPAN IN TRANSITION

Year.	Agricultural.	Mercantile.	Members of Commercial Firms and Banks.	Barristers and Public Notaries.	Journalists.	Physicians.	Government Officials.	Industrials.	Miscellaneous.
1890	144	12	14	24	12	3	27	10	5
1892	175	15	15	21	10	3	8	8	5
1894	185	15	16	24	16	1	3	7	6
1897	156	30	13	18	11	1	5	1	3

From the above it will be seen that the agricultural element has predominated in a very marked degree from the first, and that, generally speaking, it has maintained its lead; that mercantile firms have increased; and commercial, industrial, and professional members, and Government officials, have declined in numbers.

Mr. Yoshito Okuda, who was Chief Secretary of the House of Representatives, criticises the practical working of the Constitutional Government of Japan in the following words:

"Since the promulgation of our Constitution, no Cabinet has been organized without a declaration of its platform; and no Cabinet was ever in power but what failed to act up to its declaration. But that failure was passed over by the people, as if not deserving of serious consideration. No political party ever was organized here that did not issue their manifesto, but they never carried out their programme. Still the people did not blame them for this failure. Again, the members of the Diet held out some pledges to their electors, but their pledges were never fulfilled. Still society passed that over without a reproach.

"We are in a period of transition, and it is this fact that makes the smooth working of the Constitutional Government difficult at present in this country. The fault of the present state of affairs is not to be attributed to the form of government, but to the state of society at large.

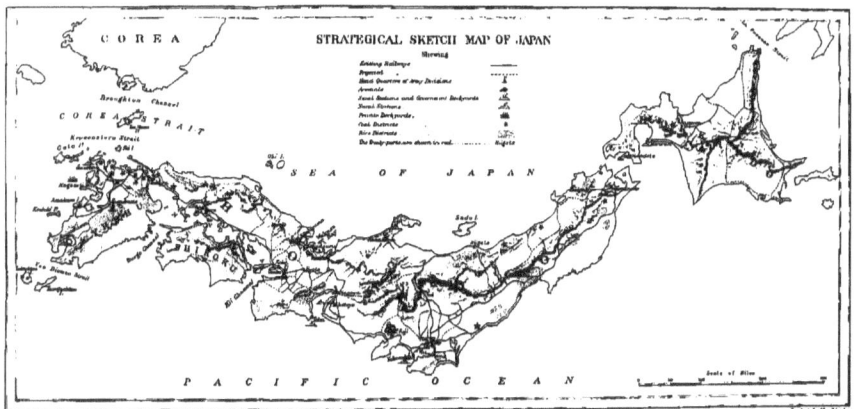

OFFICE OF THE KOKUMIN SHIMBUN (*THE NATION*, A DAILY PAPER), TOKIO

POLITICS PAST AND PRESENT

"There is another fact that impedes the smooth progress of Constitutional Government. It is the want of a proper balance in the distribution of wealth and education. In other words, the present condition of our society is such that the moneyed class in general are at a discount in point of education, while the intellectually developed are mostly deficient in wealth."

From the above it may be gathered that the political situation in Japan just now is chaotic in the extreme; and when we consider the short time during which the present form of government has been running, it is hardly to be expected that it should have been otherwise.

The full number of members of the Diet is three hundred, and they are paid a yearly salary of about £80.

Suffrage in Japan is by no means universal at the present day, as the following list of the qualifications of voters will show:

1. Male subjects of the Empire of Japan, aged full twenty-five years and upward.
2. Those who are registered in the census of, and have been residing in, the city or prefecture for full one year before the completion of the list of electors.
3. Those who have been paying in the city or prefecture a direct national tax of fifteen yen and upward per year for full one year before the completion of the electoral list, and are still continuing to pay the same; and in case of income-tax, those who have been paying the above stated sum for full three years before the completion of the electoral list, and are still continuing to pay the same.

Chamberlain estimates, presumably under the above regulations, that the number of qualified voters in Japan amounts to only "a little over one per cent. of the whole population." I think this estimate is unduly low.

Violently hostile to each other as were the conflicting parties who went to make up the Lower House, their common war-cry of " Down with the Government " at times enabled them to pull together more or less; but while, as above explained, the Government were practically unrepresented in the popular Diet, the nature of the formation of the Upper House practically assured to the Government a majority there; and, as the Higher assembly could veto any objectionable measure passed in the Lower, the position of the Government was practically so strong that one might have thought that nothing but a revolution could overthrow it. But the existence of a popular Parliament, even under these conditions, made itself felt from the first; and freedom of speech, which was granted simultaneously with the opening of the Diet, furnished another strong weapon in the hands of the Commoners.

While both Radical parties were clamoring for the destruction of the Government, neither of them had formulated any distinct policy to replace the existing methods. It was at this time that numerous other cliques were formed by dissentients from the " Liberty " and " Progress " parties, and matters began to get very complicated, the more so as every political party that sprang up had to be formally registered, after which it was forbidden by law to co-operate with any other party.

This was how matters stood at the commencement of the war with China; a Parliament without a programme, and divided against itself in every

THE OFFICE OF THE *NICHI NICHI SHIMBUN (DAY-BY-DAY* NEWSPAPER), TOKIO

POLITICS PAST AND PRESENT

conceivable way, except on the principle of thwarting the Government on all occasions. There is no doubt that the Chinese diplomatists in entering upon their war with Japan counted very considerably on the unworkable state of Japanese politics to facilitate the overthrow of that country.

On the declaration of war, however, the whole of these differences disappeared as if by magic, and the first practical proof of this was afforded when the Government at Iroshima asked the Diet in 1894 for a grant of 200,000,000 yen, and shortly after for another 100,000,000 yen for war expenditure, and both sums were accorded without a single dissentient voice.

The war taught Japan for the time being the necessity of unity in politics on broad lines, and its effect was sufficiently great to cause the " Party of Liberty " to formulate a policy and to make overtures to support the Government on a mutual basis of concession, and thus it was that the strong combination was formed between the followers of Count Itagaki and the Government, as represented by Marquis Ito and Count Inouye.

Count Okuma, however, who is looked upon by many as the strongest statesman in the country, and is certainly the most uncompromising and unbending in carrying out his policy, reverted after the war to his hostile attitude towards the Government, and strengthened the hands of his " Party of Progress " by coalescing with five other cliques, who collectively took the title Shimpo-to, which literally translated means the " Party of the Step Forward."

JAPAN IN TRANSITION

In 1896 Count Okuma succeeded in ousting the Marquis Ito, and placing this best known of Japanese politicians in Opposition for the first time since the abolition of feudalism.

Count Okuma strengthened his position by conciliating the party known as the Kokumin-to, or "National Party," of whom the best known leader was the Marquis Saigo.

This combination of cliques held the reins of Government for about a year with Count Matsukata as its nominal head. Before its dissolution, however, many changes took place, the most notable of which was the resignation of Count Okuma, who was the real motive power.

Shortly after his resignation I had the opportunity of a long interview with his Excellency at his house, on the political situation generally; and while the greater portion of our conversation had to do with international rather than with home politics, I was particularly struck with his summing up of the question as to the difference between the working of a Constitutional Government in Japan and in Great Britain.

"Your statesmen," said Count Okuma in effect, "are representing an electorate who have a definite and material point of view. The electorate is the force which guides them in their actions, and your politicians are merely the exponents of the convictions which go to make up that force. Your statesmen are pushed in their actions by that irresistible power. Your Salisbury and your Gladstone, whether

H.I.H. THE LATE PRINCE KITASHIRAKAWA
Died at Formosa when in command of the Imperial Body-guard

COUNT MATSUKATA
Twice Premier and once Minister of Finance

in power or in opposition, are well aware that their actions are backed by a real and solid community, and in consequence they can accomplish great things. We in Japan have not arrived at that stage. The people as a power are not yet behind our statesmen. We must act on our own initiative, and, however good our policy may be, it lacks the practical support of a large section of the people, that great moral force on which British statesmen can rely. As we have no general following, so we have no solid and popular Opposition, and in this we are unfortunate; for it is the existence of a powerful Opposition which calls forth the best qualities in a statesman."

This was towards the end of 1897, since which time Ministerial changes have been frequent.

At the present day the Marquis Ito and Count Itagaki are in power, and, all things considered, this powerful combination is perhaps the most satisfactory one for the country in these days of transition.

In years to come, possibly before many years have passed, with the growth of education, Japanese statesmen may obtain that popular support from the masses, which will only be forthcoming when the lower classes are in a position to understand politics in some measure.

What the popular verdict will be when that time comes one cannot tell. Will the existence of a popular voice improve matters or the reverse? Will the masses who now accept blindly the actions of their leaders be able to formulate a policy which will be any improvement on that laid down by the individuality of the chief men in the State, as at present? One cannot say.

Meanwhile Japan is lucky to possess at the head of her affairs men like Ito, Okuma, Saigo, Inouye, and Itagaki in these transition days.

Whatever may be the defects in the early working of a Constitutional Government in Japan, events have shown that when a national danger menaces the country the simple policy of patriotism, understood by all, educated or otherwise, comes to the front, smothers conflicting opinions and petty jealousies, and saves the situation in Japan—as it does in England, for the matter of that. That is perhaps the most tangible guarantee that we have that Japanese politics in the long-run will work out their own salvation; and when we study the practical effect of a Constitutional Government in Japan up to the present, and notice its weak points, we must not lose sight of the fact that its existence does not yet date back quite ten years.

THE MARQUIS SAIGO

VISCOUNT YOSHIKAWA
Minister of Home Affairs

CHAPTER XIII

OUTLINE OF STRATEGICAL GEOGRAPHY

THE number of islands which go to make up the Empire of Japan is variously estimated. In fact, one authority in giving a number very often will not come within a thousand or so of the estimate of another equally careful student of Japanese geography.

This somewhat wide disparity is not necessarily due to either authority being inaccurate in his calculations; it merely means that they differed in their opinions as to the minimum size of rock which could be reasonably dignified with the name of "island."

It is not, however, within my province to split straws on the question, as, whatever estimate we may choose to take, a glance at the map is sufficient to bring home to any one in a forcible manner the fact that Japan is made up of quite enough islands to render very difficult the problem of protecting them all adequately in time of war.

A study of Far Eastern geography should at once convince those who had considered that Japan is squandering money in a useless manner on her navy, and is unduly subsidizing and otherwise nursing her mercantile marine, that in reality in these two sections of her modern development should lie the future salvation of the country.

It is doubtless because the Japanese of to-day have realized this fact, that there are not to be found among her politicians any to correspond with our " Little Englanders." In spite of the trouble that Formosa has given the Japanese Government since they took it over, there is not a single politician who would be in favor of giving it back to the Chinese; and there is no one to suggest in a serious manner the curtailment of the naval programme.

No! This sort of " Little Japanner" has not yet been born; and, should any embryo statesman, in following out our Western methods, think that such a policy might bring him self-advertisement, he would find that the value of any notoriety thus gained would be more than counterbalanced by the fact that it would place him in a most unsatisfactory position with his countrymen.

It is to be presumed that ninety-nine out of every hundred of the Japanese islands would not be worth protecting; for the simple reason that no foreign Powers would find them worth the trouble of taking. But, if we reckon the Japanese islands by tens instead of by thousands, there still remains the fact that the task of adequately protecting such scattered and sometimes isolated pieces of territory could by no means be described as a trivial undertaking.

If Nature has ordained that Japan shall be a spread-out island-empire, and vulnerable as such, she has also

ADMIRAL NIREI

MARSHAL OYAMA
Military High Councillor, Commander of the Second Army at the time of the war with China

STRATEGICAL GEOGRAPHY

provided certain counterbalancing advantages, which help materially towards saving the situation. For, although any one of the more important Powers would have no difficulty in hoisting its flag on some of Japan's smaller outlying possessions, it is difficult to see how, except in the case of a concerted action on a large scale between the fleets of continental Europe, it could wave there for long. However, if such an eventuality were to come about, it would be of but little importance to the aggressor, except as affording him a *pied à terre* for organizing an attack on Japan proper.

"Japan proper" is usually said to consist of the three islands of Hondo, Skikoku, and Kyushu ; but for the purposes of this chapter, which deals with the defences of the country, I am assuming that Hokkaido also comes within this definition.

I cannot imagine any more inhospitable place than Japan from the point of view of an invading army; as, apart from any question of armed resistance, the geological conditions are generally such as to make it an extremely difficult country to negotiate. From the most northerly of the Kurile Islands, down to and including Hokkaido, the formation is volcanic, and the country as a rule barren. Very similar geological conditions also characterize the northern portion of the main island.

It is true that there are extensive forests in Hokkaido, but these are not of a nature to assist the invader, either in his advance or in his commissariat department. And the island is so mountainous that the advance of large bodies of troops through it would be extremely difficult at any time.

Then, again, during the winter months, that part of the country is under snow; it is always underpopulated, and, generally speaking, underfed.

Thus, even assuming that the invading army could be satisfactorily landed there, and that its presence would be of practical use in furthering the project of ultimately conquering the main island, one does not see how such an army could be fed for any length of time.

So much for the most northerly natural buffer of Japan proper.

The southern island, Kyushu, is, geologically speaking, very similar in its nature to Hokkaido. Its coast-line is extremely difficult of approach as a rule; and, once on shore, the progress of an invading army would be impeded by natural obstacles at every step.

For a variety of reasons this island would be likely to play a far more important part in a defensive and offensive war than Hokkaido.

It is true that the Japanese do not disguise from themselves the fact that Russia is their real and serious enemy, and incidentally any Powers who may be co-operating with that country.

Geographically speaking, one would expect that the direction of attack from Russia would come from the north, but bearing in mind the fact that the Russian fleet in Pacific waters at the present day would be totally incapable of coping with Japan, it

OFFICES OF THE GENERAL STAFF OF THE ARMY, TOKIO

STRATEGICAL GEOGRAPHY

is to be presumed that in the event of an attempted invasion Russian ships would have to be sent out from Europe. Consequently it is rather in the southerly portion of Japanese waters that one would expect the first encounter to take place.

It is also to be presumed that Russia would never, that is to say, within the measurable future, attack Japan single-handed with a view to invasion of Japanese territory. Thus, in event of a combined attack, one could take it that the headquarters of the fleet or fleets of Russia's co-operators would be south rather than north of Japan.

Again, it is to be presumed that Russia would never venture on open hostilities until she had practically obtained possession of the Corean peninsula; and this would also point to the south as the primary basis of hostilities.

Recent politics have shown us that Russian influence is extending in that part of the world. Holding Port Arthur and Talien-wan as she does, and pursuing a bullying policy at Peking, backed up with the practical menace of a huge military force as near to the Corean and Chinese frontiers as she can place them, and with powerful diplomatic agencies in Corea and China, we may look in the not very far-off future to the undisputed preponderance of Russian influence in Corea, unless Great Britain and Japan take measures to prevent such a catastrophe.

The extension of Russian influence in Corea is precisely what Japan does not wish for, as, if it is effected, the integrity of the Japanese Empire would be powerfully menaced.

The island of Kyushu, which, except for the smaller islands of Tsushima and Iki, is the nearest portion of Japanese territory to Corea, would seem to be the natural theatre of a future war, at all events in its early stages.

As explained above, the geological formation of Kyushu is very similar to that of Hokkaido, but it would be more advantageous to the invader in that it is prolific in rice and other food products, and is essentially the most productive coal centre in Japan.

In view of the rugged coast-line it is difficult to see, as fleets in that part of the world go at the present day, how it would be possible for Russia, or any continental European power, to effect a footing there in the face of Japan's very efficient and ever increasing naval strength.

The strategical sketch-map which will be found facing page 198 has been drawn up for the purpose of emphasizing the following features: The disposition of the various Army Divisions, Naval Stations, Government and private Dock-yards and Arsenals; those portions of the railway system, existing and projected, which touch on strategical influences; the positions of the rice and coal producing centres; and the chief mountain ranges.

In order to make this map as clear as possible, I have omitted the names and divisions of provinces and all irrelevant matter.

As far as territorial defences are concerned, the

THE IMPERIAL NAVAL DOCKYARD, YOKOSUKA

STRATEGICAL GEOGRAPHY

Japanese are equipping themselves on a scale which English people might consider excessive.

It may be taken for granted that, like our own, the Japanese Army, however efficient, could never afford a sufficient protection to the country without a proportionately strong Navy.

If Japan were to attack a foreign country, it must be by sea in the first place; and, in protecting herself from an outside foe, her primary arm must be her Navy.

Possibly Japan runs a greater risk of being invaded than Great Britain, and has consequently found it advisable to equip herself adequately to meet a force presumed to be already landed in her country; possibly, too, her present large Standing Army will be reduced in measure as the strength of her Navy increases. If there were to be a tendency to curtail the expenses in one or other of the two services, it would be the Army rather than the Navy which would first feel the effect of an economical policy on the part of the Government.

As matters stand at present, the territorial Army numbers rather over half a million men of all ranks, including about ten thousand officers.

These forces are distributed in twelve divisions, of which the respective headquarters are in the following localities: In the island of Hokkaido, Sapporo; in Hondo, Hirosaki, Sendai, Tokio, Kanasawa, Nagoya, Osaka, Fukuchiyama, and Hiroshima; in Kyushu, Kumamoto, and Kokura; and in Shikoku, Marungame.

In the three smaller islands it will be seen that all these military centres, except Kumamoto in Kyushu, are directly in touch with the railway system, such as it is in those islands.

Of the eight stations on the main island, six are on the railways—Fukuchiyama and Kanasawa being the only exceptions. Of these Kanasawa has a railway within a few miles of it, and both will shortly be connected with the rest of the railway system, as shown by the projected lines on the map.

Apart from the regular army divisions above specified, a considerable force is maintained in the island of Tsu (Tsushima), which lies half-way between Kyushu and the Corean coast, and which is rightly regarded as one of the most important strategical outposts of the Empire.

Formosa also is fairly strongly garrisoned.

From a first glance at this map it would seem that, while the Pacific side of the main island is thoroughly provided with territorial defence, the western side, which is the nearer to the Asiatic continent, is still somewhat badly equipped with railways and with military stations. It would seem too that the projected railways in this portion of the island have not been based on an ideal method from a strategical point of view, as instead of running for great distances more or less parallel with the coast, and between important centres, they have taken the form as a rule of short lines running down to the coast, at various places, from points in the interior. This unusual laying-out of the projected railways is

STRATEGICAL GEOGRAPHY

due to the irregular nature of the country, which makes it impossible to run a line of railway along the coast for any great distance at a stretch on that side of the island.

At some points along the coast the mountains run almost sheer down into the sea, thereby placing obstacles in the way, not only of the railway promoters, but of an invading force.

Another natural protection to this coast lies in the fact that along a great portion of its length it is practically unapproachable by big ships owing to the innumerable rocks and shallows.

Of the actual coast defences of the country I am not in a position to say much. The Japanese Government were very obliging in allowing me to see what I wanted to see, provided always my requirements did not clash with what they preferred my not seeing; and, as I was asked at the time not to write in a detailed manner on that subject to the papers which I was representing, I cannot very well deal with it in a book.

Suffice it for me to say that, in the opinions of naval and military expert foreigners who know the country well, the defensive strength of Japan, as far as the four principal islands and some of the others are concerned, is extremely efficient, both naturally and artificially.

It is difficult to make a comparison between the defences of Japan and those of any other country, as, with the exception of Great Britain, there is no other important insular nation whose circumstances are at all parallel; and Great Britain happens to be better protected in the way of artificial coast defence than any other country.

It is safe to say, however, that as a rule the important cities of Japan are extremely well placed from the point of view of safety against bombardment.

Tokio, the capital, lies well inside a lengthy bay, the entrance of which is protected by the most important naval station in the country—Yokosuka, which may be described as a little Chatham; while the Osaka district, the centre of industrial wealth, is protected most efficiently by the island of Shikoku and the Inland Sea.

The map shows that there are three entrances to this most beautiful stretch of water—viz., the Shimonoseki Straits, the Kii Channel, and the Bungo Channel.

Of these the first and second are strongly and quite adequately fortified, the Shimonoseki Straits being narrow, and the Kii Channel being almost spanned at one point by the island of Awaji; the tolerably wide Bungo Channel being the only weak spot. It is however expected that, at one point, the water is sufficiently shallow to permit of the erection of forts in the sea which will command the whole channel.

However, should a foreign fleet succeed in forcing this passage, it would have to solve the dual problem of threading its way through the intricate network of islands, which are difficult enough of navi-

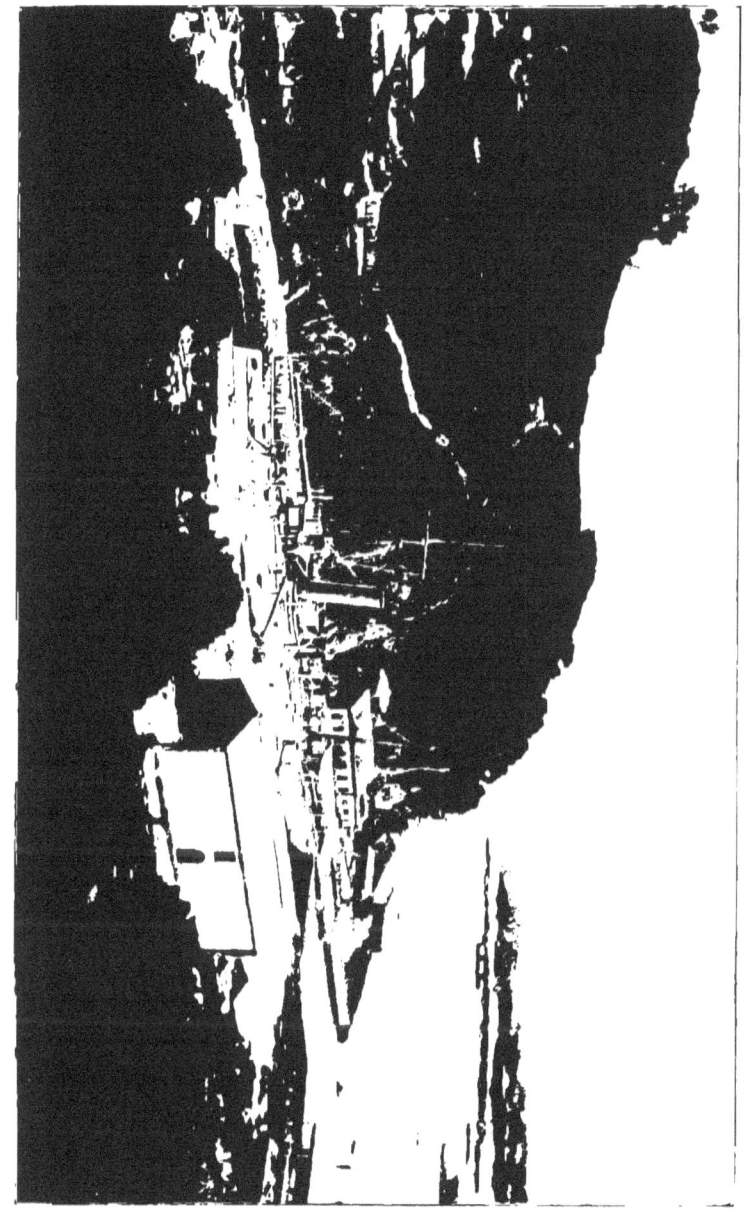

THE NAGASAKI DOCK

STRATEGICAL GEOGRAPHY

gation in times of peace, and of finding itself face to face with any force which the second naval yard of the country—Kure—could produce.

On the map the position of Nagasaki looks somewhat exposed, but as a matter of fact it lies in a sort of Norwegian fjord, the adequate protection of which is a comparatively simple matter.

At Nagasaki is to be found the best dock accommodation in Japan, in the shape of the Mitsu Bishi Dock. Here one may often see the ships of the Russian and other fleets undergoing repairs; and this fact must cause the student of Far Eastern strategy to ask himself at a very early stage of his studies where in the world any of the Powers except Great Britain and Japan would go to get their ships docked in event of a war in eastern Asiatic waters.

The growing Government Dock-yard of Sasebo is also in the neighborhood of Nagasaki.

The plant for starting the Sasebo Dock-yard was brought from Port Arthur when that place was captured by the Japanese during the war with China, and has been supplemented from time to time by machinery from Europe and America.

A fourth Government Dock-yard will shortly be established at Maidzuru on the western coast of Hondo. At that place there is a wonderful natural harbor and a good anchorage; and it is almost the only spot on that coast which can be described as at all suitable for a naval station.

On the strategical map I have shown, by black stars and red dots, the parts of the country where coal and rice are produced respectively, as these are two most important products to locate in dealing with the question of strategy.

In connection with the railway service it is of interest to note that, looked at as a means of transporting large bodies of troops at short notice, the system leaves something to be desired.

During the war with China it was found that the dislocation of the traffic due to the single-line system was a great impediment to efficient working. Then again those of our politicians who are clamoring for the suppression of the wide gauge in India and Ceylon, or at all events who would have all new lines built on the metre gauge, should bear in mind that, though the Japanese gauge is somewhat wider than that, great difficulty was experienced, owing to the fact that the carriages on their 3 feet 6 inch gauge lines were not wide enough to admit of horses standing "athwart ship" in them; thus occasioning great loss of space and time in despatching the cavalry regiments to the port of embarkation.

CHAPTER XIV

THE QUESTION OF COLONIZATION

WHEN Formosa was ceded to Japan at the close of the war with China, as a portion of the spoils of victory, there were many people who foretold that from that time forward Japan would formulate an aggressive colonial policy; and certain London papers went so far as to say that unless Japan adopted some such measure she would never realize her dream of becoming one of the Great Powers.

I confess I could not see the force of this argument, for the acquisition of colonies has not, in itself, a strengthening influence on a country. In fact, unless colonies are a necessity to a nation, their tendency is often to weaken the mother-country rather than otherwise.

If we take examples from other countries, we find that Great Britain is strengthened by her colonies because her increasing population forces her people away from home to live in other parts of the world. Thus communities are formed with a nucleus of British subjects who mean to make of such places their definite homes; and under such circumstances the British flag, in due course, finds its way there and remains planted on the spot; not protected so much by a display of arms, or by the presence of an undue number of British officials, as by the moral force created by the vested interests of the residents, backed up by a knowledge, on the part of possible enemies, that British warships can be forthcoming if required.

In the natural sequence of events, our merchant vessels find their way to such places, and the trade is mainly, but not exclusively, in British hands.

The Dutch possessions are somewhat of the same class. Such colonies pay and strengthen the hands of their mother-country.

The other side of the colonial policy is shown by France, who, with a decreasing population, holds colonies as a luxury, and because she thinks that if we possess them, she ought to show the world that she can do the same even at great cost and inconvenience.

Spain again, whose energy at the present time is not what it was, has been obliged to hand over her colonies to a more progressive nation, who may or may not find them an advantage.

The position of Spain without her colonies will probably be stronger than was the case when she had to expend large sums and many lives in endeavoring to hold on to them during the recent years of revolt.

I fancy that the Japanese colonial expansion scare had its rise in an assumption that because Britain had a large Navy and Mercantile Marine, and Japan was rapidly increasing hers on British lines, the uses

THE QUESTION OF COLONIZATION

she intended to put them to must necessarily be identical with ours. Again, no doubt, it was thought that the elation of the Japanese at the close of their war might occasion them to make a rush for colonial expansion.

After the war between Japan and China, people in Europe began to absorb a certain amount of Japanese geography, physical and otherwise, and one of the facts that the world generally began to realize was that only about twelve per cent. of the area of the whole country was under cultivation or capable of being cultivated.

We also began to appreciate that the population of Japan was a steadily growing one, and it was only natural that, under the circumstances, some of us should say that the natural remedy for this sort of thing was to be found in colonization.

There were, however, two reasons why this policy was not entered upon, and either of them was sufficient in itself to restrain Japanese colonization.

Firstly, Japan had no surplus population for colonizing purposes at the time; and secondly, there was no territory available.

With a growing population, however, and an agricultural area which has reached its limit of expansion, some natural or artificial factor must be brought in to provide the people with a means of livelihood, or the surplus population would have to leave the country.

That factor has been supplied by the vast increase in the new industries, which have not only found work for the increasing population, but have even caused a dearth in agricultural and other labor.

These industries are still multiplying, and, as pointed out in another chapter, Japan is now obliged to import much of her food from abroad.

When we add to the dearth of labor caused by these industries the further drain on the lower classes occasioned by the increase in the strength of the naval and military forces, and when we consider that the men at the head of the State, and the leading people throughout the country, still have their hands more than full with every sort of progressive undertaking at home, we shall find that the time is not yet ripe for the serious consideration of an extension of territory, even if such territory were to be available.

The Japanese have their new colony in the shape of Formosa, and this in itself has offered more than enough in the way of problems for solution to statesmen and students of colonial policy for the time being.

The only outward and visible sign which the Japanese gave which might seem to indicate that they had a notion that some day they might wish to extend their empire was afforded by the organizing of a Colonial Department, with a Colonial Minister at its head. Such a department was not necessary under the circumstances, and the Government quickly realized that fact.

Possibly its being started was due to that spirit of megalomania which we so often hear about; but

THE QUESTION OF COLONIZATION

at all events, whether this was so or not, from the moment it was considered to be unnecessary the Government took no half measures, such as curtailing expenses and calling the department by a less high-sounding name. They merely suppressed it, with that suddenness which characterizes so many of their important changes—that suddenness which makes Japanese politics so difficult to follow, and an attempt to describe them satisfactorily so disheartening.

When Russia, France, and Germany combined to prevent Japan from annexing Corea after the war, they deprived her of the only portion of the mainland of the Asiatic continent which would have made her a suitable colony or which she coveted; certainly, too, it was the only portion of the mainland which she stood a probable chance of being able to hold.

Her reasons for desiring to possess Corea were substantial and logical. Firstly, Corea had already a large Japanese population; secondly, as long as it was under Chinese protection, the progressive policy adopted by the Japanese, and essential to her newly born line of action, could not be brought to bear in that country; thirdly, its possession would have strengthened Japanese influence at Peking, an influence which would at once have been healthy, friendly, and in the interests of civilization; fourthly, Japan considered, rightly or wrongly, that Corea would have formed an advantageous "buffer" territory against Russian aggression in North China.

It is to be presumed that England and America, at all events, would have been glad to see Corea in the hands of the Japanese, even from a purely selfish point of view; as apart from the purpose of opening up that peninsula, and the improvement in international commerce which would have been entailed thereby, it would mean that we should have had a very powerful moral, if not actual, ally in Japan. With so great a stake in the mainland of that part of the world Japan would have been obliged, had the necessity arisen, to have borne most of the brunt of such warfare as might be entailed in opposing Russia's aggressive policy—a policy which we profess to deplore and even to resent, but which, apparently, we do not see our way to check.

Whether Japan would have been strong enough to hold her own against Russia in Corea, had the occasion arisen, I do not profess to know. It has been said that, though Japan might carry on a successful sea and land war against the Chinese, the situation would be reversed if she were to find herself face to face with a white enemy.

How far Russians in that part of the world are to be considered "white" is a matter of opinion; but one thing we do know, and that is that the extension of Russian territory—in Asia, at all events—has not as a rule been occasioned by actual force of arms, but by a display of strength, backed by judicious and extensive bribery.

It is an open secret that the success of Russian policy in North China has been due to the diplo-

THE QUESTION OF COLONIZATION

macy of the "palm," and that his Excellency, Li Hung Chang, has been among the largest recipients of largesse from St. Petersburg.

The smoothing of the palm policy has been, whenever the occasion demanded it, alternated with that of the shaking of the fist; in other words, by the massing of troops in the nearest available territory. But it has never come to blows.

Russia's policy on the Afghan frontier has been precisely of a similar nature; and there royalty, in the shape of the Ameer's son, is said to have succumbed to the practical pecuniary blandishments of Russia.

Turning to Europe, we find that Russia has conquered and absorbed Finland, and portions of Poland and Turkey. Of these victories, one may say that in Turkey Russia had to face an enemy who, at the time, was about as badly organized and unprepared as the China of to-day might prove. In Finland, which in some geographical features bears, with regard to Western Russia, a certain resemblance to Corea in the East, Russia also had to deal with a powerless foe, against whom she was able to concentrate the best of her energies, as the country to be conquered was situated conveniently for her purpose.

Of Poland it is safe to say that Russia would never have conquered it single-handed; and that she only effected her portion of the victory after terrible losses, and because Germany and Austria were simultaneously attacking the Poles on their

JAPAN IN TRANSITION

other frontiers, so that they could not devote anything like their whole attention to resisting the Russians.

Of the two defensive wars worth mentioning where foreign armies have invaded Russian territory—that is to say, the Crimean War and the Napoleonic Invasion—Russia was defeated in the former instance; and gained the day in the latter, not by fighting, but by running away, burning her own towns and cities, and allowing the *Grande Armée* to starve and freeze itself to death.

This was a victory, no doubt, but not a victory of arms—a victory rather determined by length of leg, length of country, and length of winter.

My reason for dealing so fully with Russian warfare in a chapter on Japanese colonization is that it is necessary to show that, if it is Russia who has checked Japan in the past, so it will be Russia who will leave no stone unturned to do so in the future. Japan at the present day is far too advanced in civilization to be a welcome neighbor to Russia, whose policy, therefore, is to keep her at arm's-length.

All the events referred to above happened a long time ago, some of them a very long time ago; and the greatest optimist with regard to Russia's military strength would find it hard to deduce from them that they have afforded a practical proof that her prowess and capabilities are of an overwhelming nature in the actual field of battle, except in so far as numerical strength is concerned. Have we any right to assume that in facing the armies of to-day

THE QUESTION OF COLONIZATION

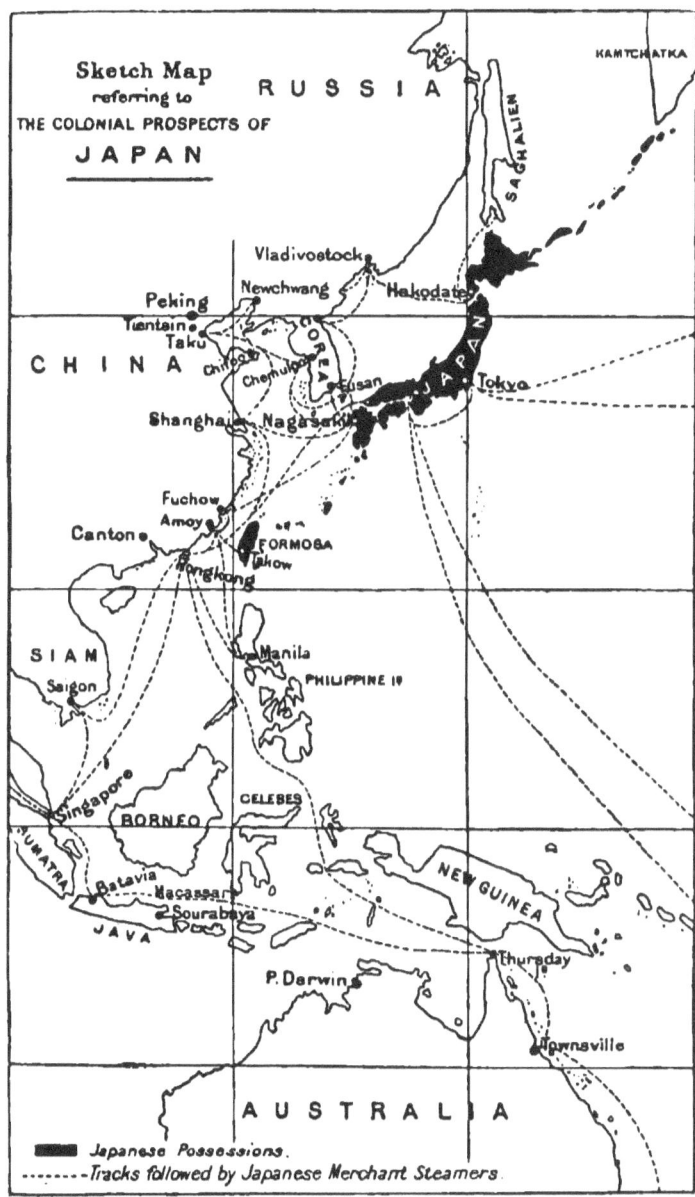

JAPAN IN TRANSITION

she would be able to do better than she did in times gone by?

Experts in strategy tell us that Corea is not an easy country to invade from the land, and that there appears to be no reason why a well organized, if comparatively small, defending army should not be able to hold its own against very heavy odds. It is for this reason that Japan, if once properly installed in that peninsula, might possibly defend it against Russia, if it were a question of coming to blows; and Russia would have no possible chance against Japan in attempting an invasion by sea.

At the present day this discussion may be considered to be of a somewhat academical nature, inasmuch as Japan is not now in possession of the Corean Peninsula. So many people, however, maintain that Japan is to become a colonizing nation, that it is necessary to make some reference to the territory which would seem, for many reasons, to be the most natural one to form a substantial Japanese colony, and for the possession of which Japan, at all events, made a strong if ineffectual bid.

A glance at the map on the preceding page will suffice to show that, whatever the force which was able to keep Japan out of Corea may have been, that same influence could be brought to bear with greater strength to prevent her acquiring any other territory on the Chinese coast; so that for the time being, at all events, we may dismiss from our mind the idea that Japan will endeavor to colonize on the Asiatic continent.

THE QUESTION OF COLONIZATION

Then comes the question as to the direction in which one should look to find the probable colonizing area of Japan, if she is destined to have one.

At one time people took it into their heads that Japan wanted to annex the Hawaiian Islands, situated half-way between her and America.

I do not think that she ever seriously contemplated this step. Although I was living in Japan during the acute period of the Americo-Japano-Hawaiian question, and was in touch with politicians, diplomatists, and journalists there, I can only say that I saw and heard nothing that could be twisted into meaning that Japan had any designs on these islands.

She wished merely to protect the interests of Japanese subjects living there; and when America first talked of annexing Hawaii, Japan's one and only thought was to make sure that her subjects should have, at all events, as much fair play as they had had when the islands were governed by an Independent Republic *pour rire*. Possibly the attitude she assumed on the occasion when she thought her interests were menaced was rather an aggressive one, and occasioned some friction between herself and the United States; but, roughly speaking, she finished by getting more or less what she required.

Her main fear was that under American rule there might be a tendency to treat the Japanese in Hawaii as the Chinamen are treated, for obvious reasons, in the United States. She also feared that the McKinley and Dingley Tariffs would be applied to the detriment of Japanese commerce.

The number of Japanese emigrants to Hawaii has been habitually much exaggerated. There was an impression to the effect that these islands have formed the great recipient of the surplus population of Japan. When I explain, however, that the total number of Japanese residents in Hawaii amounts to about 24,500, and that there are sufficient births in Japan every year to people the entire Hawaiian group three times over with a number equal to their existing total population of various colors (about 110,000 people all told), it will be seen that, either the existence of these islands as an outlet for Japan's surplus population is without importance, or that Japan's surplus population is very small.

My theory, as stated at the commencement of this chapter, is that, in view of the rapidly increasing industrial field in Japan at the present day, the surplus population in that country may be treated almost as a *quantité négligeable*, and that for some time to come it will remain so.

Going farther afield than Hawaii, and dropping for a moment the question of colonies in the political sense of the word, it is well to point out that strenuous efforts have been made during recent years to colonize industrially some of the western shores of Mexico with Japanese.

Syndicates and companies, owning Mexican territory, have been energetically working in Japan for the purpose of getting agriculturists to go to Mexico, and to carry on farming and other industrial enterprises.

THE QUESTION OF COLONIZATION

The leading statesmen in Japan have been approached on the subject; and in the beginning the sympathies of some of them were enlisted in these schemes. One or two such colonies were actually started, but I believe I am right in saying that they have not turned out satisfactorily; although one of the Ministers of Agriculture and Commerce —I think it was Viscount Yenomoto—worked very hard to make the first of them a success.

It is generally admitted that island colonies are, as a rule, more easily acquired and more easily retained than is the case with portions of territory on the mainland of a continent.

If this theory is accurate with regard to countries generally, it would seem to point to the assumption that Japan, an empire composed of islands, and having extensive naval and commercial fleets, should find in islands the natural extension of her possessions. It is said, too, that colonies strike downward from the mother-country as a rule—that is to say, that the mother-country usually lies in a more northerly latitude than her dependencies. Throughout the world there are only just a sufficient number of exceptions to prove the general validity of this rule.

Thus, geographically and strategically speaking, it would seem that, if Japan is to acquire further colonies, her future field would lie among the innumerable islands of the Southern Pacific.

This part of the world would also seem to be indicated by the fact that it is there that the Japanese trader and artisan are finding their way when they leave their country; and another significant argument in favor of this view is afforded by the rapidity with which these seas are becoming more and more thoroughly worked by the Japanese merchant ships.

Already, as far south as the northern shores of Australia, the Japanese communities are beginning to make themselves felt as a factor, and an increasing one, in the population of many of the islands which intervene between Formosa and Australia.

The map shows us that the present Empire of Japan stretches in one lengthy and fairly straight line of islands, without any very wide gaps between them, from Kamtchatka on the northeast down to a point on a line drawn between Hong Kong and the Philippines on the southwest. The effect of such a position is that, given a sufficiently powerful fleet, Japan would be in a very formidable position for holding the seas, as far as preventing intercourse with the Russian and Chinese seaboard is concerned.

Generally speaking, people have not grasped the situation that, while Japan's primary object in increasing her naval strength is self-protection, her ultimate aim is to make herself so powerful in Far Eastern waters that her voice will perponderate in international questions in that part of the world.

Pending the realization of that dream, it is difficult to see where her new colonies are to be found, as although there are hundreds of small islands which could almost be had for the asking, all the larger ones which are worth having are held by nations

THE QUESTION OF COLONIZATION

with whom it would not answer Japan's purpose to go to war now; and who would not part with them at a price which it would be worth Japan's while to pay.

Assuming that such islands were in want of a tenant, Japan's natural area for colonial extension would be the Philippines, the Moluccas, and New Guinea, as by appropriation there she would lengthen her protective chain along the east of Asia.

But as matters now stand, to acquire those islands Japan would have to deal, amicably or otherwise, with the United States, Holland, Britain, and Germany.

At present she is not able to offer any sort of *quid pro quo* in exchange for these; but were she to become overwhelmingly powerful in those waters, so powerful, in fact, that her services could be utilized to further other ends of the various nations who own those places, there is no telling to what extent the ownership of the islands in the Southern Pacific might change hands.

We, who are accredited with holding on to our possessions, have before now ceded to the Dutch and the Germans more valuable territory than the British portion of New Guinea, for instance, for a return far more inadequate than would be afforded by the co-operation of the Japanese naval and military forces in, for example, enforcing our supremacy in the Yangtse Valley.

There has been some talk of the Americans disposing of certain of the Ladrone group to Japan for a consideration; and it is possible that, had the war between Spain and America taken place five or ten years later than it did, the Japanese might have gone in with the United States in her attack on the Spanish possessions, and have shared the spoils in the shape of the Philippines.

Before leaving the subject altogether, it is as well to say a few words as to the one existing colony possessed by the Japanese—Formosa.

While all sorts of side lights, many of them unfavorable, have been thrown on the methods adopted by the Japanese in colonizing Formosa, there has never been a full and unbiassed account by a foreigner. Most of the reports which have found their way into the European press have emanated from missionary sources, and have been prejudiced, sensational, and often misleading.

The reason for this is to be found in the fact that the missionaries, however conscientious, have by their actions, at all events during the early stages of the occupation, materially increased the difficulties which beset the Japanese in endeavoring to establish their rule.

To understand matters it must be borne in mind that the Japanese are not Christians. Now, their policy in Formosa from the outset was based on what is known as "toleration," and in following this out they did not interfere with the religious views of the natives, except in cases where these views entailed, as they sometimes did, the perpetration of the most horrible atrocities.

THE QUESTION OF COLONIZATION

The business of the missionaries was to Christianize the Formosan savages, a process with which the Japanese did not interfere. So far so good; but the missionaries, in their laudable zeal for the cause, found it incumbent on them to preach the doctrine to their followers that the religion of the Japanese was a worthless one, and in some instances they entered into the political arena against them.

It speaks well for the Japanese that, however galling such an action might be to them, and however much the effect of discrediting their religious views might tend to lower their prestige in the eyes of the natives, they did not take forcible measures to put a stop to this, from their point of view, injurious propaganda.

There is no doubt, however, that some of the regrettable incidents which occurred between the Japanese soldiers and the people of the country were due to the feelings of the natives having been worked upon by the missionaries in this way.

No doubt, in endeavoring to settle the country on its new basis, blunders of policy were made, and at times unnecessary blood was spilt. I do not think, however, that, bearing in mind the condition of the country and the savage nature of the people, the sum total of these "atrocities," as they have been called, exceeded those which might have been expected of almost any other nation placed in a similar position.

It must be remembered that the handing over of Formosa to the Japanese did not mean putting them in peaceful possession of a law-abiding community, which had been governed by any sort of civilized rule. In practice, the ceding of Formosa by China to Japan meant really that the European Powers acquiesced in Japan taking possession of the island and subduing and reducing to order the inhabitants, comprising between two and three millions of the most dangerous type of Chinamen — a variety of mixed breeds, in which the Papuan negro, the Mongolian, and the Malay predominated—and a multitude of lawless and hitherto untamed savages of the most desperate nature.

The Japanese are being guided in their Formosan policy by ours in India. They are altering the native laws and customs as little as possible, and, as above stated, leaving the people their religion. They are establishing the Japanese language, and certain military officers hold a sort of go-as-you please roving commission to experiment in making soldiers out of the tribesmen. If the results of these preliminary trials seem hopeful, organized steps will be taken to deal with the matter on a large scale.

The inter-racial hatred which existed so strongly in India, and helped us materially in establishing our position there, found its equivalent to some extent in Formosa in the hatred which has always existed between the natives and the Chinese population.

As an illustration of the extent to which the Formosan natives are uncivilized, it is interesting to note that on one occasion the Governor-General, in pursuance of the policy of toleration, caused a mes-

THE QUESTION OF COLONIZATION

sage to be conveyed to certain of the chiefs to the effect that the new rulers would endeavor to respect the native customs, and suggesting that if they had any reasonable requests to make, the Japanese authorities would be willing to fall in with their views. The tribal chiefs, after consultation, said that they were very happy under the new state of affairs, but they had one request to make—viz., that as a certain number of Chinamen's heads were essential to the proper carrying out of their religious ceremonies, and under the new conditions it was becoming increasingly difficult to obtain them, they would be much obliged if the Japanese, who now had the upper hand, and consequently greater facilities, would kill the necessary number of Chinamen and send them the heads at the time required for the propitiation of their gods.

In spite of the sensational reports to the contrary, the policy of the Japanese in Formosa has, on the whole, been logical, lenient, and careful, and there has been nothing whatever in their methods so far to lead one to imagine that they will be incapable of dealing with colonial matters in the future.

When I was living in Tokio I had the advantage on several occasions of talking with Baron Nogi, who was at that time the Governor-General in Formosa, with his aide-de-camp, and with his secretary. I was shown several letters from European residents in Formosa, expressing thanks for and approval of the methods he had employed in carrying out his uphill task of producing order out of chaos.

Among the difficulties to be met with in Formosa may be mentioned a pestilential climate, cutthroat and hostile inhabitants, squalid and filthy villages, lofty and inaccessible mountains, the most prolific rainfall, and consequently most extensive floods in the world, an occasional earthquake, and a varied assortment of insect life in its most unpleasant form.

From the above it will be seen that any country about to embark on a scheme of colonial expansion could not possibly have had a better practical school in that way than has been afforded to Japan by Formosa, which in a compact space contains representative samples of almost all the problems which the colonist is likely to have to face, except at the North Pole.

Under the circumstances we need not be hypercritical with regard to Japanese colonial methods, if they have not succeeded after less than five years of occupation in converting such a pandemonium into a paradise.

But, as stated earlier, Japan is not greedy for more colonies at the present day; and perhaps, after all, Russia may be said to have inadvertently conferred a great benefit on her neighbor when she forced her to relinquish Corea. For had Japan continued to occupy that country she would have been obliged to maintain a very large military force there, which would have been an extremely serious

THE QUESTION OF COLONIZATION

drain on her already overtaxed resources ; whereas as matters now stand she is able to spend all her available capital on her navy, to which she rightly looks for the solution of the question as to what her influence on the world's history is to be in the future.

CHAPTER XV

JAPAN AS AN ALLY

AMONG the many sensational rumors that of recent years have been floating about the world on the subject of Far Eastern politics, not one has been more persistent, and at the same time more vague, than that which accredited Great Britain and Japan with having "arrived at an understanding." In diplomatic language "an understanding" is a very convenient and comprehensive term. It may mean anything between a definite and binding political alliance and a loosely made arrangement to adopt certain parallel lines of policy under certain conditions.

The " understanding " between Great Britain and Japan was not, in any sense of the word, of a formal nature, and yet its moral strength was so great that the mere knowledge of its existence has been enough on more than one occasion lately to prevent the breaking out of what would have been the most serious war of modern times. Its strength did not lie in signed documents, for such documents did not exist and were not needed; nor had it a foundation either on bluff or on that bogus sentiment which has formed the basis of certain international understandings.

The fact of the matter is that the trend of politics in the Far East has of late years had the effect of driving English and Japanese interests into channels which, if not altogether identical in theory, are very much so in practice.

It is only during the last year or two that certain Powers became aware that if they persisted in pushing an aggressive policy in the Far East beyond a certain point there would come a time when neither England nor Japan would allow such a state of affairs to go on. The only result to be expected from such an eventuality would be that England and Japan must act in concert to check such aggression. The allied fleets of these two countries would have no difficulty in becoming masters of the seas and the coast-lines in that part of the world.

In dealing with the question of a possible Anglo-Japanese alliance one must run over in a brief way some of the salient points with regard to recent international politics in the Far East; and this necessitates my departing to some extent from the policy laid down in this book of dealing with Japan only; for China has been, of course, the principal political arena.

Speaking generally, the vital interests of Great Britain in China are centred in the Yangtse Valley; except that Peking, being the seat of the Government of that country, it is essential to our policy that we should retain, not only a ready access to that city for diplomatic purposes, but that we should be able to make our strength felt there; for that is the only way to retain influence in China.

JAPAN IN TRANSITION

Otherwise the portion of China over which it is essential that our influence should be paramount lies between the Shantung promontory on the north and the Canton River on the south. North of the Gulf of Pechili no possible combination of the forces of other nations could check Russia's slow but steady advance through Mongolia and Manchuria in her policy of absorption of Northern China. Nor would such an advance by Russia through northern inland China be detrimental to British interests, provided British influence at Peking were not to be depreciated thereby. As long as Peking continues to be the political capital of China it is therefore essential to our policy that Russia's acquisitions should not reach southward as far as that capital.

The Chinese have a saying to the effect that China is a mulberry leaf, and Russia the worm which is devouring it piece by piece. There is no doubt that Russia is doing, and will do, her best to fulfil the functions of the worm in question; but a certain amount of time is necessary, in the natural course of things, to allow her to go through the processes of swallowing and properly digesting the various morsels. That Russia should absorb the coast-line of Northern China and of the Corean Peninsula is dead against the interests of both Britain and Japan. Japan is sufficiently harassed with Russia as a near neighbor at the present day, and does not in any way wish an extension of Russian seaboard in her immediate vicinity. The reason why it is not in Britain's interests that Russia should be extended in this manner is, that we have no wish that Russian influence should be forced on Japan. There is no doubt that England and Japan, in combination, could readily check Russia's advance along the coast, and even keep her out of the Corean Peninsula altogether.

From time to time we are told that England and Russia are on the point of coming to an understanding about matters in China, and if such an understanding could be arrived at it would be a very excellent thing to accomplish; but the lines of policy of the two countries are so entirely at variance, and our experience of understandings with Russia has been so unsatisfactory, that it is not in the least probable that any workable scheme, with this end in view, could be brought about. Again, it is difficult to see how any such scheme could be otherwise than detrimental to the interests of Japan, who is our natural ally, for the time being, in that part of the world.

Of late, too, Germany has become a factor in Northern Chinese and Japanese politics by her acquisition of Kiao-chau, and this fact has a strong bearing on Anglo-Japanese relations. It has become our policy, quite recently, to avoid hurting German susceptibilities, as far as possible, in our press, and, no doubt, such a policy is a praiseworthy one. But we must not lose sight of the fact that in occupying a portion of the Shantung Peninsula Germany acted under the immediate protection of

Russia, whose policy it was to let anybody, rather than England, gain an ascendency in that part of the world. The fact that Russia, by treaty with China, had a prior claim to the occupation of Kiao-chau, was not emphasized in the press at the time; and, when it was mentioned, the point of view taken was usually that Russia was performing a graceful Mother Hubbardly action in the nature of " giving the poor dog a bone"; otherwise, that she was raising no objection to Germany, who had faithfully backed her up in preventing the Japanese from reaping the advantages of their war, acquiring a tardy reward for her services.

At that time Germany's attitude was distinctly antagonistic to British interests; and if it is less so now, and if the Germans have become our *bona fide* friends in Far Eastern matters, the mystery as to the cause of this change of front is not hard to explain. The reason lies in the fact that Wei-hai-wei is now in the hands of the British, and that, without Wei-hai-wei, the strategical value of the Shantung Peninsula is practically *nil*. Thus the object of the Germans in taking Kiao-chau, unless they remain on friendly terms with the holders of Wei-hai-wei, has been negatived.

Kiao-chau by itself is practically useless either as a strategical or commercial centre, and it was taken by Germany merely as forming the thin edge of the wedge, in a policy which was eventually to take the form of commanding the southern entrance to the Gulf of Pechili. This could only be done by means

JAPAN AS AN ALLY

of Wei-hai-wei, and the German dream was that, after establishing themselves in the peninsula with a fairly large territorial army, they would be the natural people to take possession of that place when the Chinese had paid off the balance of their war indemnity, and the Japanese had, in accordance with their treaty, evacuated it.

The taking over of Wei-hai-wei by the English was the smartest diplomatic stroke that we have accomplished of late years in the Far East; and in bringing it about, those who could read between the lines had an opportunity of seeing, for the first time, that we were morally aided and abetted by Japan. At this time, and without any warning, Japan began to press China to pay off the balance of the war indemnity; and this was effected by means of an arrangement in which Great Britain played an important role; with the result that we stepped into the occupation of Wei-hai-wei, without any sort of resentment on the part of the Japanese, but to the undisguised wrath of Russia, and to the consternation of Germany.

But our acquisition of Wei-hai-wei is only an advantage to us as a strategical centre in so far that it enables us to hold one of the sea keys to Peking, and as affording us a certain power of restraining Germany in adopting an exclusive commercial policy in that part of the world. In the first flush of the acquisition of their new colony there is no doubt that it was the intention of the Germans to adopt such a method. For, while they stated that Kiao-chau was to be an open port, they had in effect hedged round their compact with the Chinese with a variety of conditions, the putting into force of which would have practically stopped the possibility of the people of any other country carrying on a satisfactory trade there.

As practical people, however, they have, now that the English hold Wei-hai-wei, come to the conclusion that to reap any benefit from their colony they will have to work with Great Britain, for the time being, at all events.

Our alleged prospects of an understanding with Russia and our peaceful arrangements with Germany in the Far East are based on foundations which may give way at a moment's notice; for when all side issues are done away with, the fact remains that Russia must be Britain's most important political enemy in that part of the world, and that Germany is our most inveterate commercial opponent. Of the other two countries with whom we have to reckon in Far Eastern politics, the United States and France, the former cannot at the present day be looked on in any other light than that of a country whose sympathies and interests are identical with our own, and on whose moral co-operation, at all events, we could reckon in case of need; whereas France, whose interests are essentially confined to Southern China, would no doubt be friendly enough to Britain were it not for the fact that unfortunate events of recent occurrence in other parts of the world have had the effect of estranging French

VISCOUNT KATSURA
Minister of War

MARSHAL NOZU
Superintendent General of the Eastern Military Section,
Commander of Fifth Division during the war with China

sympathies from us. Therefore, until such time as France shall have realized the one-sided nature of the bargain she has made with Russia, she can hardly be numbered among the militant friends of Great Britain in the Far East.

Thus it is that England might have to face at any time in that part of the world the allied strengths of Russia, France, and Germany; which, as far as maritime warfare is concerned, would not be a very terrible ordeal, provided that Japan were neutral and the United States a sympathetic on-looker. If, however, Japan were to throw in her lot with Russia and Germany against Britain, matters would, of course, be very different.

But in the natural course of things such an eventuality could not take place unless Russia and Germany were powerful enough to force Japan into an alliance. Extreme pressure would be required for this, as Japan, who dislikes foreigners generally, has a greater horror of Russia, politically speaking, than of any other nation.

By a strange fatality, too, Germany is Japan's greatest commercial opponent. For while it is mainly British and American machinery which Japan is importing for the purposes of her new industries, she is turning out by the means of such machines goods which compete with German rather than with British products. It would seem, therefore, that political events are tending to throw Great Britain and Japan, and possibly the United States, into each other's arms in the Far East, and then comes the question as to the feasibility of a co-operative arrangement between these countries.

There is no doubt that Japanese statesmen recognize fully the political and commercial strength of the Anglo-Saxon race; and there is no doubt that as Westerners go the Japanese have a greater respect for them than they have for the people of any other countries.

At the same time the Japanese are Asiatics, and remain Asiatics at heart; and they resent the fact that Westerners of any sort should decide the destinies of nations in that part of the world. This very natural feeling was expressed to me by more than one politician, and very emphatically by that most astute of Japanese statesmen Count Okuma, who looks upon China as the natural ally of Japan. That this opinion is shared by those who guide the politics of that country has been proved very clearly to the world lately by the visit of Count Okuma's great political rival, the Marquis Ito, to Peking, on the subject of Chinese reform.

The eventual ideal of the Japanese is that Japan and China together should be able to satisfactorily deal with Far Eastern matters, as opposed to the ever encroaching Westerner. Japan perfectly realizes the impossibility of making an ally of China as matters now go, but her ardent wish is to see the bringing about of an enlightened China with whom a serious compact could be made. How long that dream will take to realize can only be a matter for conjecture; but pending such time the sympathies of

Japan must go out to such of the "Western barbarians" as are most likely to enhance the prospects of such a scheme; and Japan has very rightly come to the conclusion that the Anglo-Saxons are the only people who do not wish to interfere with such a policy. Whether English and American people are studying their own eventual interests in endeavoring to educate and enlighten and Christianize the Asiatics is quite another matter; but that we go to continual enormous expense to effect this object is beyond question.

Russia, of course, boasts that her success in acquiring and successfully holding her extensions of territory in Asia is mainly due to the fact that she not only does not endeavor to educate the natives in such territory, but that she makes it more impossible than ever for them to improve their condition in any way, by encouraging them to retain everything which is barbarous that they have, and by hemming them round with that terrible official grip, which the unfortunate natives find far more onerous than their own laws. It has been my lot to visit, besides Russia proper, various territories which have been conquered, or have otherwise come under the "protection" of Russia in Europe and in the Far East, and the bitter hatred against Russia in such places is universal and extreme; but there can be no doubt as to the efficacy of the Russian system from their point of view. The Japanese are aware of this, and the system does not in the least appeal to them. It is against Russia, her immediate and powerful neighbor, that the modern Japanese armaments are directed at the present day. Germany and France are also naturally looked upon by Japan with distrust, from the fact of their co-operation with Russia, above referred to, at the close of the war with China.

These, from the Japanese point of view, are the reasons why Japan looks with a comparatively friendly eye on the English and the Americans of the present day, for she feels that were Russia, France, and Germany in combination strong enough to enforce their will with regard to Far Eastern matters, the political and commercial prospects of Japan would be ruined once and for all.

Another thing which would be certain in such an eventuality is that with the ruin of Japan the ruin of British prestige and trade in the Far East would come simultaneously; and it is for these reasons that it would be in the interests of both these nations to support each other's policy.

As an ally, Japan would be at once a powerful and a loyal co-operator. Imbued with pluck, determination, and endurance, and with a rapidly growing knowledge of modern warfare and its methods, there is no ally from the British point of view in that part of the world who could compare with Japan. Together, as far as naval warfare is concerned, England and Japan could at the present day hold the position against all comers; and the interests and authority of these two countries could be maintained entirely by means of naval warfare. Neither wishes to acquire territory in Russia or in

Central China, and, in the event of war, their energies could consequently be entirely devoted to dealing with the ships and holding the coast-line of the enemy. In fact, as matters now stand, Japan and England could, by playing a somewhat waiting game after hostilities had begun, bring about a coal famine which would cripple the whole of their opponents, including Russia, if the season of the year were well chosen.

CHAPTER XVI

OUR PROSPECTS UNDER THE REVISED TREATIES

By the time this book is published we shall be within a few months of the coming into force of the revised treaties between Japan and the outside world. Of the sweeping changes which will take place when the new treaties do come into force, the chief will be the abolition of the extra-territorial rights of resident foreigners on the one hand, and the nominal throwing open to the foreigner of the whole of the Empire of Japan for purposes of travel, trade, residence, and the leasing of land and premises, on the other.

In order clearly to explain what our extra-territorial rights in Japan amount to, I quote the words of that great academical authority on the institutions of that country, Mr. Basil Hall Chamberlain:

"... If an Englishman commits a theft, he is tried, not by a Japanese judge, but by the nearest British consular court. In civil cases where one party is a Japanese and the other a foreigner, the suit is carried into the court of the defendant's nationality. If I want to sue a Japanese, I must sue him in a Japanese court; but a Japanese sues me in a British court. A corollary to this is that the interior of Japan remains closed to foreign residence and foreign trade—even to foreign travel except with passports—it being evidently undesirable that a country should harbor persons not ame-

OUR PROSPECTS UNDER REVISED TREATIES

nable to its laws. Foreigners are therefore restricted to Yokohama, Kobe, and the other 'Treaty-ports.'

"Extra-territoriality, claimed thirty years ago as the only *modus vivendi* which could render the existence of civilized Christian beings endurable in the Japan of those days, has since then been violently assailed by some as unjust to Japan, whose independent sovereign rights it is held to infringe. Thus, the partisans of extra-territoriality found their arguments on alleged practical utility, whereas its opponents reason deductively from considerations of abstract right. Meantime, in view of Japan's frank adoption of European culture, the controversy has been closed by surrender on the foreign side. According to treaties recently concluded, all foreigners will come under Japanese law about the close of the century."

Resident foreigners very naturally do not at all relish the prospect of coming under Japanese jurisdiction, after having enjoyed their extra-territorial rights for over thirty years. But our *quid pro quo* is, as above explained, the throwing open of the country to us. There are people who maintain that this last privilege amounts to nothing in reality, as we have for some years past enjoyed the privilege of travelling all over Japan, provided that we were armed with a passport, easily obtainable, and the formalities respecting which did not entail any trouble, provided that we could produce it when required.

As matters stand, until the revised treaties come into force, the foreigner is allowed to travel without his passport only within the limits of a circle having a radius of 24½ miles round the various treaty-ports, and to reside only in certain specified concessions within these limits.

Not only, however, can one travel all over the country with a passport, as mentioned above, but by going through the formality of taking a nominal employment under a Japanese subject, any fairly well-behaved foreigner can obtain permission from the Government to reside in almost any part of the country.

We cannot, however, carry on a trade, commerce, or industry outside treaty limits. But even this event is to be got over, when required, by simply carrying on such trade in the name of a Japanese friend. When such a course is adopted, the business in question belongs in practice as well as in theory to the Japanese man of straw; and, as explained earlier in this book, if such a man should turn out to be dishonest, his European partner cannot make good any claim against him for defalcation.

It speaks well for that Japanese business morality, which is so often maligned, that a partnership on these lines could be carried on at all under such conditions, and I am bound to say that I have heard of very few cases where the Japanese have taken unfair advantage of their position.

The most striking instance of Japanese abusing the confidence of foreigners who had reposed this sort of trust in them was afforded by those converts to Christianity referred to in a previous chapter; who, as soon as they considered themselves strong enough in the knowledge of their new faith to conduct it in their own manner, turned out the American missionaries who had founded, built, and organized the "Christian University of Kioto." This, however, can hardly be classed as a commercial

OUR PROSPECTS UNDER REVISED TREATIES

fraud, as, although it is very usual in Japan for missionaries to mix Christianity with commerce, this particular college was not a trading concern.

Although it has been possible under existing circumstances to find certain Japanese subjects sufficiently honorable to make it worth the while of the foreigner to use them as nominal partners, and to set up his business in the interior while having no legal rights, it stands to reason that the revised treaties which will give the foreigner the power to work such a business on his own account, and on an equal footing with the people of the country, will afford an incentive to foreign enterprise in this direction which has never yet existed.

There are people who maintain that the clauses of the treaty as regards tenure of land by the foreigner are so unsatisfactorily worded that they will not offer any inducement to him to embark his capital in industrial enterprises. I do not hold this opinion myself, because I am quite sure that under the new treaties the foreigner in Japan will be vastly better off under Japanese jurisdiction than he is in a dozen other countries where he successfully employs his capital in this manner.

This much disputed question as to the possibility of extension of trading and industrial facilities represents, I take it, almost the only available asset in the way of a tangible advantage which the foreigner has gained by his new treaties with Japan. Such as it is, we, as Englishmen, cannot claim to have secured it; for though, as foreign interests go in

Japan, the British interests preponderate over all the others, it was we who, being the first to conclude an imperfectly considered treaty with Japan, irrevocably damaged the prospects of our fellow-countrymen at present residing in that country.

The example afforded by Britain was more or less promptly followed by other countries, and all the important Powers signed treaties of a similar nature with Japan. Fortunately for us, however, some of the other Governments, notably those of France and Germany, looked into the matter rather more closely than we did, and insisted on certain of the more glaring defects in our treaty being partially rectified in theirs; and of course we benefit by such modifications under "the most favored nation clause." The fact, however, of Great Britain having actually signed her ill-considered treaty on certain lines hampered the action of the other Powers, by making it much more difficult for them to insist upon important alterations.

The result of this has been that Japan's diplomatic victory over all the civilized Powers of the world has been in many ways more decisive and important than her strategical victory over China.

When Lord Kimberley signed our revised treaty with Japan in 1894, the voice of the "Little Englander" was more powerful than it is to-day. The consequence was that the strong protests of our compatriots in the treaty-ports of Japan against the wording of the treaty were, to the everlasting disgrace of our Home Government, unheeded.

OUR PROSPECTS UNDER REVISED TREATIES

Once more I would quote from Mr. Chamberlain's book, where, in a postscript on the subject of " Treaties and Treaty Revision," he holds out the following appalling estimate of our prospects :

> "As the date for the enforcement of the treaty draws near, and men have to make arrangements accordingly, they find themselves confronted with obstacles which could never have arisen had the negotiators exercised ordinary foresight. The ambiguity of the document is not the least of its defects. A careful consideration of what was not stipulated for, as well as what was, shows that under the new treaty British subjects may not improbably lose their privilege of publishing newspapers and holding public meetings—in a word, their birthright of free speech ; and that it is doubtful whether their doctors and lawyers will be allowed to practise without a Japanese diploma. Even the period for which leases can be held was left so uncertain as to have become the subject of endless controversy; the conditions of the sale and repurchase of leases, in what had hitherto been the foreign "concessions," were left uncertain; the right to employ labor and to start industries was left uncertain. With things in this state, with the great English steamship companies, the P. & O. and Canadian Pacific, probably prevented from carrying passengers between the ports, and with new duties of from 30 to 40 per cent. levied precisely on those articles which are prime necessities to us but not to the Japanese, could any one imagine such terms having ever been agreed to except as the result of a disastrous war."

While there is no doubt that Mr. Chamberlain is perfectly justified in what he says in regard to the unsatisfactory nature of this treaty, and while our Government was guilty of culpable negligence in not considering all the points now raised before concluding the treaty, I cannot help thinking that many writers have taken an unduly pessimistic view of our prospects under tne new regime.

It is premature, and possibly wrong, to assume that the Japanese will be so ill-advised as to endeavor to render the position of the foreigner untenable in Japan, for the simple reason that their own interests must, in the long-run, lie in the opposite direction.

Undoubtedly it was high time for extra-territoriality to be abolished in Japan. British subjects stand in far greater need of such rights in any of the South American Republics, the Transvaal, Spain, Portugal, and Russia, than they do in Japan at the present day; and yet our business men live and thrive in all those countries, and generally speaking, it would seem that our Government is capable of efficiently safeguarding our interests abroad.

To sum the matter up, it may be said that, in concluding our new treaty with Japan, we have done the right thing, but have done it wellnigh as badly as it could have been done. Now that it is concluded and past reconsideration, its theoretical side is not so important as the practical question as to how we shall stand in Japan when once these treaties come into force.

English business men in Japan, as a rule, are strong in their opinion that the treaties will ruin them, and many of them will doubtless look upon the criticisms on which I have ventured above as being vastly too mild. But I cannot help feeling that the dismay of such people as to their future prospects is mainly due to the fact that most of them have never known other conditions of trade, and that they attach too much value to the wholesome, but sometimes misleading conviction, that satisfactory trade can only be carried on under British legislation.

The *Japan Gazette* has constituted itself the champion of the malcontents in this way, and, while it has no doubt done some good in pointing out certain weak features in the new treaties, it has sometimes adopted so exaggerated a tone that were this journal to be read outside Japan its statements would prove very misleading, both as regards the actual provisions of the treaties and the spirit in which these clauses are intended to be read. Local people, however, who read the paper in question, are able to make allowances for these exaggerations, and to form their own opinions accordingly.

The effect of the aggressive tone on the part of some of the foreign treaty-port journals on the subject of treaty revision has been to awaken a somewhat similarly hostile attitude in the Japanese press. In consequence of this, a bitterness and acrimony which are greatly to be deplored have been imported into these delicate questions, the satisfactory solution of which can only be brought about by calm and reasonable discussion.

Thus on the one side we learn from treaty-port papers that our rights of carrying on trade are to be abolished; our houses are no longer to be our castles; we are to be subject to every conceivable annoyance and inconvenience at the hands of the Japanese officials; we are to be robbed, squeezed, black-mailed, etc., with impunity, and dragged before an unjust tribunal, conducted by Asiatics whose only notion of meting out justice to the hated Westerner will be to suppress him by fair means or foul.

We are told that we must fight against this sort of oppression. I should think we must, if it were to exist. We must teach the Japanese that a successful war with an effete nation like the Chinese does not enable them to ride roughshod over the rights of the white man, and so on, and so on. This is the gist of the treaty-port logic, as far as the journals are concerned; and it is all very well as far as it goes. It appertains to that ever-popular style of cheap patriotism of the "Britons never shall be slaves" class, which, however sound in itself, loses much of its point when the alleged opposing party has neither the wish nor the power to reduce us to that unfortunate condition.

All this, however, has had the effect of causing certain fiery Japanese orators to talk of "enforcing" the conditions of the new treaties; and agitations have been set on foot with a view of determining the best method of carrying out such "enforcement." If the exaggerated views propounded by these ultra anti-foreign politicians were to be put into effect the practice of the working of the new treaties would not at all accord with the theory of those who framed them.

Thus a great deal has been said on both sides which with advantage might have been left unsaid, and it is a cause for satisfaction to find that, as a rule, the responsible politicians and diplomatists who

OUR PROSPECTS UNDER REVISED TREATIES

will have to see to the proper carrying out of this delicate task of making the change have not been influenced by the views of the extremists on either side.

In spite of all the alarmist theories, the unprejudiced man, who has had any experience of the world in general, cannot make up his mind to be vastly uneasy as to the way in which the new treaties will operate.

They may be in many ways unsatisfactory, no doubt they are; but it is either too late or too early to talk much of that now; for, even if there were a serious wish to alter them on one or other side, there is not the slightest probability as to their being modified now until they have had a fair trial.

Certain local foreigners seem to hold the opinion that with the abolition of our extra-territorial rights our political influence in Japan will be, *ipso facto*, abolished with them. But it is to be presumed that our diplomatic and consular staff will be perfectly able to safeguard the interests of our people living in Japan.

As pointed out in another chapter, the Japanese legal code is an excellent one; the men who govern in that country are, as a rule, level-headed and competent; they enforce their laws equitably and without unduly oppressive measures being taken, and they are beginning to recognize that the foreigner, however little they may like him as an institution, is, at all events, a necessity—a necessity, that is, to the fulfilment of their progressive international policy.

Another and often unnoticed phase of this question is that, while we (the foreigners) are bitterly complaining of the hardships we are to suffer on account of these treaties, the Japanese on their part do not consider that the throwing open of their country will by any means be an unmixed blessing to them.

The possession of extra-territorial rights by the foreigner has for years past been a thorn in the side of Japanese self-respect, and in order to have this abolished, they consider that they have given a very substantial *quid pro quo* in admitting the foreigner to all parts of their Empire on an equal footing with themselves.

The Japanese are said to wish to obtain all the advantages of the opportunities afforded by our civilization without incurring any of its drawbacks; they would have foreign capital without an increase in foreign influence; and they would have foreign trade without the foreign trader. All this may be very natural, though it is undoubtedly unreasonable. But until the Japanese have solved the difficult problem of "having their pudding and eating it" they will not be able at once to modernize themselves and blot out the foreigner and his influence.

Thus it is that they are opening their country to us; but they are doing it with very great reluctance.

No doubt in its initial stages the forthcoming régime may fall very heavily on certain individual traders, for the conditions of trading will of necessity be revolutionized.

The great and overwhelming advantage, alike to

OUR PROSPECTS UNDER REVISED TREATIES

Japanese and to foreigners, to be found in the provisions of the treaties, lies in the fact that life under the new conditions will enable each to know more of the other, as international intercourse will be less restrained. It is to be hoped that the result will be that both will learn to know and respect the other more than at present.

If such is to be the case, both sides will have cause to congratulate themselves; and, whatever may be the eventual solution of the modern policy of the Japanese nation, it is to be sincerely hoped that British and Japanese interests may remain as they are at present—practically identical.

Let us hope, too, that in adopting so many of our Western methods, they will never allow to die out the many excellent qualities which characterized the Old Japan, that Japan which we are so often told no longer exists—the Japan of Mitford and Lafcadio Hearn; a far more æsthetic and possibly more virtuous country than the one it has been my lot to write about as "Japan in Transition."

THE END

www.ingramcontent.com/pod-product-compliance
Lightning Source LLC
Chambersburg PA
CBHW030744250426
43672CB00028B/395